THE ENCYCLOPEDIA OF PSYCHOACTIVE DRUGS

SERIES 1

SERIES 2

WHO USES DRUGS?

GENERAL EDITOR
Professor Solomon H. Snyder, M.D.

*Distinguished Service Professor of
Neuroscience, Pharmacology, and Psychiatry at
The Johns Hopkins University School of Medicine*

•

ASSOCIATE EDITOR
Professor Barry L. Jacobs, Ph.D.

*Program in Neuroscience, Department of Psychology,
Princeton University*

•

SENIOR EDITORIAL CONSULTANT
Joann Rodgers

*Deputy Director, Office of Public Affairs at
The Johns Hopkins Medical Institutions*

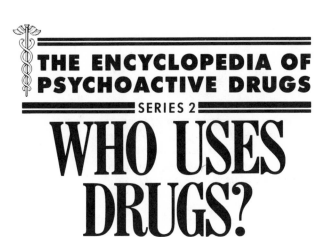

THE ENCYCLOPEDIA OF PSYCHOACTIVE DRUGS

SERIES 2

WHO USES DRUGS?

PETER GWYNNE

CHELSEA HOUSE PUBLISHERS
NEW YORK • NEW HAVEN • PHILADELPHIA

*A note regarding the pictures in this book: Unless
specifically stated in captions or text, none of the people
in this book are involved in the use of illicit drugs or
the misuse of legitimate drugs. No picture in this
volume is intended to suggest—nor should it be taken
as suggesting—substance abuse on the part of those
pictured.*

EDITOR-IN-CHIEF: Nancy Toff
EXECUTIVE EDITOR: Remmel T. Nunn
MANAGING EDITOR: Karyn Gullen Browne
COPY CHIEF: Juliann Barbato
PICTURE EDITOR: Adrian G. Allen
ART DIRECTOR: Giannella Garrett
MANUFACTURING MANAGER: Gerald Levine

Staff for WHO USES DRUGS?

SENIOR EDITOR: Jane Larkin Crain
ASSOCIATE EDITOR: Paula Edelson
ASSISTANT EDITOR: Michele A. Merens
EDITORIAL ASSISTANT: Laura-Ann Dolce
COPY EDITOR: Ellen Scordato
ASSOCIATE PICTURE EDITOR: Juliette Dickstein
PICTURE RESEARCHER: Susan Hamburger
DESIGNER: Victoria Tomaselli
DESIGN ASSISTANT: Donna Sinisgalli
COVER ILLUSTRATION: Liane Fried

CREATIVE DIRECTOR: Harold Steinberg

3 5 7 9 8 6 4 2
Library of Congress Cataloging in Publication Data

Gwynne, Peter, 1941–
    Who uses drugs?
    (The Encyclopedia of psychoactive drugs. Series 2)
    Bibliography: p.
    Includes index.
    1. Drug abuse—United States—Juvenile literature.
[1. Drug abuse] I. Title. II. Series.
HV5825.G89 1988   362.2′93   87–13259

ISBN 1-55546-223-5

CONTENTS

Drug abuse pervades American life in the 1980s. It has cost society billions of dollars in lost productivity and treatment expenses and has scarred millions of lives.

In the Mainstream
of American Life

One of the legacies of the social upheaval of the 1960s is that psychoactive drugs have become part of the mainstream of American life. Schools, homes, and communities cannot be "drug proofed." There is a demand for drugs — and the supply is plentiful. Social norms have changed and drugs are not only available—they are everywhere.

But where efforts to curtail the supply of drugs and outlaw their use have had tragically limited effects on demand, it may be that education has begun to stem the rising tide of drug abuse among young people and adults alike.

Over the past 25 years, as drugs have become an increasingly routine facet of contemporary life, a great many teenagers have adopted the notion that drug taking was somehow a right or a privilege or a necessity. They have done so, however, without understanding the consequences of drug use during the crucial years of adolescence.

The teenage years are few in the total life cycle, but critical in the maturation process. During these years adolescents face the difficult tasks of discovering their identity, clarifying their sexual roles, asserting their independence, learning to cope with authority, and searching for goals that will give their lives meaning.

Drugs rob adolescents of precious time, stamina, and health. They interrupt critical learning processes, sometimes forever. Teenagers who use drugs are likely to withdraw increasingly into themselves, to "cop out" at just the time when they most need to reach out and experience the world.

9

A pharmacist displays the variety of prescription drugs on the market. These drugs are often effective pain or anxiety relievers, but some of them can be addictive and physically destructive.

Fortunately, as a recent Gallup poll shows, young people are beginning to realize this, too. They themselves label drugs their most important problem. In the last few years, moreover, the climate of tolerance and ignorance surrounding drugs has been changing.

Adolescents as well as adults are becoming aware of mounting evidence that every race, ethnic group, and class is vulnerable to drug dependency.

Recent publicity about the cost and failure of drug rehabilitation efforts; dangerous drug use among pilots, air traffic controllers, star athletes, and Hollywood celebrities; and drug-related accidents, suicides, and violent crime have focused the public's attention on the need to wage an all-out war on drug abuse before it seriously undermines the fabric of society itself.

The anti-drug message is getting stronger and there is evidence that the message is beginning to get through to adults and teenagers alike.

The Encyclopedia of Psychoactive Drugs hopes to play a part in the national campaign now underway to educate young people about drugs. Series 1 provides clear and comprehensive discussions of common psychoactive substances, outlines their psychological and physiological effects on the mind and body, explains how they "hook" the user, and separates fact from myth in the complex issue of drug abuse.

Whereas Series 1 focuses on specific drugs, such as nicotine or cocaine, Series 2 confronts a broad range of both social and physiological phenomena. Each volume addresses the ramifications of drug use and abuse on some aspect of human experience: social, familial, cultural, historical, and physical. Separate volumes explore questions about the effects of drugs on brain chemistry and unborn children; the use and abuse of painkillers; the relationship between drugs and sexual behavior, sports, and the arts; drugs and disease; the role of drugs in history; and the sophisticated drugs now being developed in the laboratory that will profoundly change the future.

Each book in the series is fully illustrated and is tailored to the needs and interests of young readers. The more adolescents know about drugs and their role in society, the less likely they are to misuse them.

Joann Rodgers
Senior Editorial Consultant

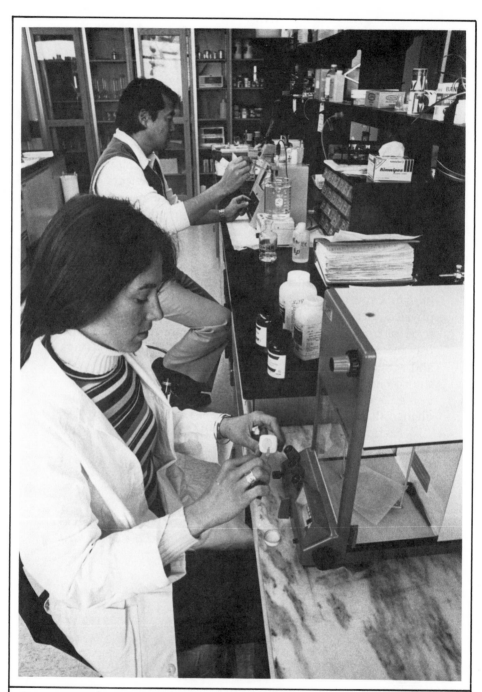

Drug research and manufacture is a multi-billion dollar industry and has led to the development of sophisticated medicines. Ironically many drugs meant for healing can also be abused.

INTRODUCTION

The Gift of Wizardry
Use and Abuse

JACK H. MENDELSON, M.D.
NANCY K. MELLO, Ph.D.
Alcohol and Drug Abuse Research Center
Harvard Medical School—McLean Hospital

Dorothy to the Wizard:

"I think you are a very bad man," said Dorothy.
"Oh no, my dear; I'm really a very good man; but I'm a very bad Wizard."
—from THE WIZARD OF OZ

Man is endowed with the gift of wizardry, a talent for discovery and invention. The discovery and invention of substances that change the way we feel and behave are among man's special accomplishments, and, like so many other products of our wizardry, these substances have the capacity to harm as well as to help. Psychoactive drugs can cause profound changes in the chemistry of the brain and other vital organs, and although their legitimate use can relieve pain and cure disease, their abuse leads in a tragic number of cases to destruction.

Consider alcohol — available to all and yet regarded with intense ambivalence from biblical times to the present day. The use of alcoholic beverages dates back to our earliest ancestors. Alcohol use and misuse became associated with the worship of gods and demons. One of the most powerful Greek gods was Dionysus, lord of fruitfulness and god of wine. The Romans adopted Dionysus but changed his name to Bacchus. Festivals and holidays associated with Bacchus celebrated the harvest and the origins of life. Time has blurred the images of the Bacchanalian festival, but the theme of drunkenness as a major part of celebration has survived the pagan gods and remains a familiar part of modern society. The term "Bacchanalian Festival" conveys a more appealing image than "drunken orgy" or "pot party," but whatever the label, drinking alcohol is a form of drug use that results in addiction for millions.

The fact that many millions of other people can use alcohol in moderation does not mitigate the toll this drug takes on society as a whole. According to reliable estimates, one out of every ten Americans develops a serious alcohol-related problem sometime in his or her lifetime. In addition, automobile accidents caused by drunken drivers claim the lives of tens of thousands every year. Many of the victims are gifted young people, just starting out in adult life. Hospital emergency rooms abound with patients seeking help for alcohol-related injuries.

Who is to blame? Can we blame the many manufacturers who produce such an amazing variety of alcoholic beverages? Should we blame the educators who fail to explain the perils of intoxication, or so exaggerate the dangers of drinking that no one could possibly believe them? Are friends to blame — those peers who urge others to "drink more and faster," or the macho types who stress the importance of being able to "hold your liquor"? Casting blame, however, is hardly constructive, and pointing the finger is a fruitless way to deal with the problem. Alcoholism and drug abuse have few culprits but many victims. Accountability begins with each of us, every time we choose to use or misuse an intoxicating substance.

It is ironic that some of man's earliest medicines, derived from natural plant products, are used today to poison and to intoxicate. Relief from pain and suffering is one of society's many continuing goals. Over 3,000 years ago, the Therapeutic Papyrus of Thebes, one of our earliest written records, gave instructions for the use of opium in the treatment of pain. Opium, in the form of its major derivative, morphine, and similar compounds, such as heroin, have also been used by many to induce changes in mood and feeling. Another example of man's misuse of a natural substance is the coca leaf, which for centuries was used by the Indians of Peru to reduce fatigue and hunger. Its modern derivative, cocaine, has important medical use as a local anesthetic. Unfortunately, its increasing abuse in the 1980s clearly has reached epidemic proportions.

The purpose of this series is to explore in depth the psychological and behavioral effects that psychoactive drugs have on the individual, and also, to investigate the ways in which drug use influences the legal, economic, cultural, and even moral aspects of societies. The information presented here (and in other books in this series) is based on many clinical and laboratory studies and other observations by people from diverse walks of life.

Over the centuries, novelists, poets, and dramatists have provided us with many insights into the sometimes seductive but ultimately problematic aspects of alcohol and drug use. Physicians, lawyers, biologists, psychologists, and social scientists have contributed to a better understanding of the causes and consequences of using these substances. The authors in this series have attempted to gather and condense all the latest information about drug use and abuse. They have also described the sometimes wide gaps in our knowledge and have suggested some new ways to answer many difficult questions.

One such question, for example, is how do alcohol and drug problems get started? And what is the best way to treat them when they do? Not too many years ago, alcoholics and drug abusers were regarded as evil, immoral, or both. It is now recognized that these persons suffer from very complicated diseases involving deep psychological and social problems. To understand how the disease begins and progresses, it is necessary to understand the nature of the substance, the behavior of addicts, and the characteristics of the society or culture in which they live.

Although many of the social environments we live in are very similar, some of the most subtle differences can strongly influence our thinking and behavior. Where we live, go to school and work, whom we discuss things with — all influence our opinions about drug use and misuse. Yet we also share certain commonly accepted beliefs that outweigh any differences in our attitudes. The authors in this series have tried to identify and discuss the central, most crucial issues concerning drug use and misuse.

Despite the increasing sophistication of the chemical substances we create in the laboratory, we have a long way to go in our efforts to make these powerful drugs work for us rather than against us.

The volumes in this series address a wide range of timely questions. What influence has drug use had on the arts? Why do so many of today's celebrities and star athletes use drugs, and what is being done to solve this problem? What is the relationship between drugs and crime? What is the physiological basis for the power drugs can hold over us? These are but a few of the issues explored in this far-ranging series.

Educating people about the dangers of drugs can go a long way towards minimizing the desperate consequences of substance abuse for individuals and society as a whole. Luckily, human beings have the resources to solve even the most serious problems that beset them, once they make the commitment to do so. As one keen and sensitive observer, Dr. Lewis Thomas, has said,

> There is nothing at all absurd about the human condition. We matter. It seems to me a good guess, hazarded by a good many people who have thought about it, that we may be engaged in the formation of something like a mind for the life of this planet. If this is so, we are still at the most primitive stage, still fumbling with language and thinking, but infinitely capacitated for the future. Looked at this way, it is remarkable that we've come as far as we have in so short a period, really no time at all as geologists measure time. We are the newest, youngest, and the brightest thing around.

WHO USES DRUGS?

Police raid a secret drug lab in a doctor's house. Drug abuse within the medical profession is a widely acknowledged problem; this doctor was accused of selling for profit the drugs he manufactured.

CHAPTER 1

DEFINING THE PROBLEM

Who uses drugs, and what substances do they use and abuse? Certainly, there is no "typical" participant in drug activity in the United States. Users include the teenager nervously puffing on his or her first marijuana joint at a party, the film star free-basing cocaine after a long day on the set, the skid row bum begging for a quarter to help buy liquor, and the physician secretly injecting himself with fentanyl, a powerful and dangerous synthetic anesthetic.

It is not clear what persuades individuals to start and continue using drugs. All that psychologists agree on is that the motivations are complex and interlinked. Some experts say that cocaine and other drugs simply make users feel good about themselves. That is a powerful reason, especially for people who feel rather inadequate under normal circumstances. Also, it is generally agreed that a number of sociological factors contribute to a climate tolerant of widespread drug abuse. There have been pervasive, not always positive changes in American values and social arrangements since the late 1960s, resulting in a society that celebrates instant gratification and too often shuns all but facile solutions to even the most difficult problems. The influence of traditional "small-town" values has been undermined by the growing

A pipe used to smoke crack. The use of this highly addictive crude form of cocaine is a problem of epidemic proportions in the 1980s and has spurred a nationwide antidrug movement.

mobility of Americans. Moreover, a general spiritual malaise seems to have set in among many of the nation's most talented and affluent members, stemming from rampant careerism and materialism and a corresponding decline in more traditional moral and spiritual priorities.

Although there may be no single explanation for the current epidemic of drug abuse, or any single model for the typical drug abuser, there is a valid perception on the part of the public that chemical dependency has reached crisis proportions. Men and women of all ages and from every walk of life are affected in both their personal and working lives; the nation's productivity suffers. The country's youth, already at risk in destabilized families and communities, is particularly vulnerable to the potentially lethal effects of drug and alcohol dependency.

A National Response

The public and media began to respond most strongly to the issue of drug abuse in the early 1980s when crack, a particularly cheap, dangerous, and addictive form of cocaine, appeared on the streets. The new drug represented yet another threat to the health of American adults and children. Moreover, a startling series of deaths of various public figures and celebrities during this period crystallized public apprehensions about drug use and availability. Up-and-coming basketball star Len Bias, well-known comedian John Belushi, and David Kennedy, son of the late senator Robert Kennedy, all fell victim to substance abuse in the 1980s, and their deaths were covered extensively by the media.

Between March and October 1986, the NBC television network ran 400 separate reports on drug use and abuse. *Newsweek* and *Time* magazines devoted cover stories to the topic of drug abuse. Spearheaded by first lady Nancy Reagan, a nationwide "Just Say No" campaign featuring well-known

In 1985 Nancy Reagan attended a First Ladies conference on drug abuse. The international gathering, which was sponsored by the United Nations, highlighted the need for a worldwide war against drugs.

celebrities encouraging children to shun drugs and alcohol appeared frequently on radio, television, and in the press. Public officials became vocal supporters of the war against drugs, proclaiming their support for federal and statewide drug abuse programs.

By the end of 1986 the barrage of publicity given to the dangers of chemical dependency had begun to make its mark on the public's consciousness. Public health professionals had begun to identify the types of drug problems that existed in different segments of society, the areas where these problems were most prevalent, and the reasons why drug use among Americans continued at a high and steady rate. Commented A. M. Rosenthal, executive editor of the *New York Times*, in *Time* magazine, "This is not a press-created problem, nor a crisis made by politicians. Drugs are here."

What Are the Facts?

Much of the understanding of the drug culture and its influence on American life is anecdotal, but some organizations regularly collect data on this issue. The most highly regarded statistics are probably those compiled by the federal govern-

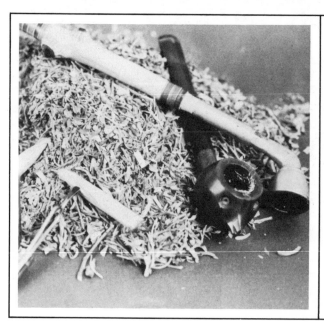

Marijuana entered the American mainstream in the 1960s. In spite of increasing evidence that it is hazardous to health, this psychedelic drug is still widely used.

ment's National Institute on Drug Abuse (NIDA). These figures indicate three major facts about drug use in the United States in the 1980s:

•The use of most drugs remained steady or declined slightly during the first half of the decade;

•Use of cocaine increased significantly during the same period;

•The number of Americans using illegal drugs was extremely high during the 1980s.

Furthermore, studies by Lloyd D. Johnston of the Institute for Social Research at the University of Michigan include these statistics:

•About 30% of current college students will have used cocaine at least once before they graduate;

•By their middle twenties, 80% of today's young adults will have used an illicit drug other than marijuana;

•Only in recent years have high school and college students perceived any serious risk in using cocaine;

•Men are more likely than women to use illicit drugs.

The Gateway Drug

Before 1960, the number of high school seniors who reported using marijuana daily was virtually zero. By 1979 that figure had soared to 11%. To put these percentages into proper focus, NIDA released a National Household Survey on Drug Abuse revealing actual estimated numbers of marijuana users in the country in 1982. The survey reported the following statistics for the early 1981–82 period:

•Close to 20 million Americans were current users of marijuana; that is, they had used the drug within the past month;

•Approximately 31,400,000 Americans had used marijuana within the past year;

•About 56,300,000 (including current users) had used the drug at least once.

More recent figures indicate that by the mid-1980s, about 6 million Americans used marijuana on a daily basis, despite increasingly negative information about the drug's side effects. Studies indicated that, for example, smoking marijuana could cause more potential lung damage than cigarette smoking.

Marijuana use also poses a less direct but potentially much more serious threat to the individual and society. According to William Pollin, former director of NIDA, many experts regard marijuana as the key "gateway" drug that leads to abuse of more dangerous substances. "In recent years," Pollin has written, "the best single predictor of cocaine problems in a given individual has been how early and how heavy that person's use of marijuana has been."

Cocaine and Heroin

In the 1980s, cocaine emerged as the major illicit drug of abuse. According to surveys, the number of users in the United States increased by more than one third between 1982 and 1985, from 4.2 million to 5.8 million. The number of users suffering harmful side effects from the drug, measured by such criteria as visits to hospital emergency rooms and deaths as a result of overdoses, increased even more rapidly during that period.

The addictive properties of cocaine have been demonstrated in animal experiments. Studies have consistently shown that cocaine is the single drug that animals do not have to be trained to use, and that they will choose it over food and water to the point of starvation or dehydration.

Heroin retains its popularity as a drug offering a false but seductive sense of euphoria. Heroin is almost always administered by injection into the bloodstream and rapidly produces a potent but potentially debilitating "high." From 1969 to 1974, according to NIDA, the number of heroin addicts in the United States more than doubled, from 242,000 to 558,000. In the mid-1970s, more than 650 residents of New York City alone were dying as a result of heroin abuse each year. A decade later, the state of New York was treating 31,000 heroin-addicted individuals with methadone (a substance that blocks the effects of heroin withdrawal but that is in itself addictive). Government estimates put the number of heroin addicts in the United States in the mid-1980s at half a million.

Heroin use did start to decline in the 1980s, however, for two major reasons. One was the emergence of cocaine as an illicit drug of choice; the other was the realization that the transmission of acquired immune deficiency syndrome (AIDS) was linked with the sharing of AIDS-contaminated needles by drug addicts.

Nevertheless, while heroin abuse among the entire population may be on the decline, increasing numbers of cocaine addicts have begun to use it as a means of countering the brutal depression that follows a cocaine high. Entertainer John Belushi died after an injection of a mixture of the two, a lethal "cocktail" known as a speedball.

Other Popular Poisons

Marijuana, cocaine, and heroin are the "big three" of the illicit drug world, but other illegal substances continue to tempt and threaten Americans. Amphetamines, popularly known as speed, may temporarily stimulate the individuals who use them, but can also kill those who use them to excess. Fentanyl and a host of other sophisticated synthetic anesthetics are obtained easily by some medical professionals who use drugs to function under pressure.

After a period of decline following their heyday during the 1960s, the use of hallucinogenic drugs, such as LSD, is once again on the rise in the nation's high schools and colleges. PCP, a drug known on the street as angel dust, which can stimulate or depress the user's feelings according to the individual's personality, the environment, and the dosage, continues to plow its own sad furrow. And in the early 1980s, enterprising chemists in basement laboratories began inventing "designer drugs" — synthetic substances related closely enough to illicit psychoactive drugs to induce similar effects in users, yet different enough to remain legal until authorities could identify and classify them. Designer drugs represent in many ways the ultimate in dangerous drugs. Users have no guarantee of their purity, or even if they are pure, of their side effects. In fact, one such drug, a synthetic

25

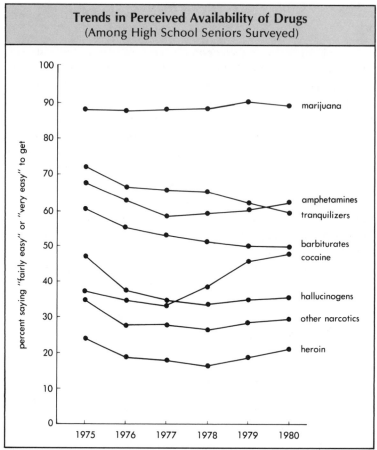

Trends in Perceived Availability of Drugs
(Among High School Seniors Surveyed)

percent saying "fairly easy" or "very easy" to get

marijuana
amphetamines
tranquilizers
barbiturates
cocaine
hallucinogens
other narcotics
heroin

1975 1976 1977 1978 1979 1980

Table 1

heroin, was discovered to cause irreversible symptoms of Parkinson's disease, a deterioration of the nervous system that normally occurs only in elderly people.

As indicated in Table 1, a deadly assortment of illicit drugs is readily available on the streets. This chart, published in 1981, showed that high school seniors were finding such drugs as marijuana almost universally obtainable. Significantly, cocaine, which has been seen until recently as an expensive drug available to people with money and status, was viewed by 48% of high school students as being readily available to them as well.

The Most Accessible Drug

Of course the most accessible drug for all age groups remains alcohol, a result of its legality and at least tacit acceptance in society. Alcohol also remains the most dangerous drug for the majority of the population, largely because of the carnage wrought by drunken drivers on the nation's highways.

Here are the tragic facts of alcoholism: Drunk drivers kill approximately 25,000 people each year on American highways and injure 750,000 more. The National Council on Alcoholism estimates there are 10 million to 13 million alcoholics and problem drinkers in our society. Alcohol is often considered a drug that can be mixed with other psychoactive drugs to achieve more immediate and long-lasting effects. This is a false notion. According to Paul Quinnett, author of *The Troubled People* (1982), approximately 2,500 American lives are lost each year as a result of lethal drug and alcohol interactions.

Though statistics may vary slightly from year to year, it is evident that almost all Americans — young or old, rich or poor — have access to drugs and a significant number frequently abuse them. In the following chapters we will examine in detail the phenomenon of drug use among specific segments of American society; the many reasons why individuals turn to drugs, and how this dependency affects their lives; and describe efforts that are being made to solve the myriad problems created in a society permeated with drugs.

The busy floor of the New York Stock Exchange. Cocaine abuse has been a serious problem in the fast-paced financial community where salaries are high but stress is often overwhelming.

CHAPTER 2

DRUGS IN THE WORKPLACE

A sting operation by police in San Jose, California, the city at the center of the Silicon Valley computer components industry, led to an astonishing revelation. Of a work force of 400 people in one company, 90% were using drugs.

In retrospect, however, perhaps this discovery should not have been surprising at all. In a region defined as affluent and fast-paced, drugs can be as much a part of the scenery as expensive cars and designer clothes. *The Big Score: The Billion Dollar Story of Silicon Valley* (1985), by Michael S. Malone, describes the situation: "Drugs are everywhere in Silicon Valley. Alcohol is the most easily abused. The number of alcoholics in boardrooms on executive row is shocking. But increasingly, just as common and far more apt, given the local lifestyle, is cocaine. Silicon Valley has become a coke blizzard." Malone goes on to say that the Drug Enforcement Agency cites Silicon Valley as a center of cocaine abuse in the United States.

Well-paid computer experts are not the only fast-track careerists for whom drugs are a way of life. Manhattan's Wall Street brokerage and financial services firms are notorious for high rates of cocaine and other drug use among their associates. Incidents of drug use, particularly of cocaine, among these professionals have been well documented; several large and prestigious brokerage firms now periodically test new employees for substance abuse.

Certainly cocaine seems to attract up-and-coming young professionals in many fields. According to "End of the Line," a program produced by WNBC television in New York, 1 in 7 cocaine users in early 1987 earned more than $50,000 per year. "The new morality of young America is success," declared Ralph Whitehead, a professor at the University of Massachusetts, in *Time* magazine. "Pot bred passivity. On alcohol a person can't perform well. But cocaine fits the new value system. It feeds it and confounds it. Young adults walk a tight line between high performance and self-indulgence, and cocaine puts the two together."

Blue-collar Workers

Highly paid employees in Silicon Valley or on Wall Street may be indulging in expensive drugs while on the job, but drug use is by no means confined to workers who can afford these habits. On-the-job addiction belongs to no class, color, or occupation.

General Motors Company, for example, identified serious drug problems in many plant workers at its facilities and set up several sting operations with undercover agents to combat the problem. In the summer of 1986, 10 GM workers were caught in a drug and gambling ring in Michigan. And the 1972 book *The World of the Blue-Collar Worker*, edited by Irving Howe, further documented the problem of drug abuse on the job. Said Sam Bellomo, a vice-president of Chrysler's Local 7 union, "Boredom on the job? The speed up? That's routine. What workers fear most is the drug addict in the plant. They [the workers] worry about the safety of operations and they dread knowing that pushers operate in the plants and their victims work there."

Case Histories

How do these harrowing statistics on substance abuse in the workplace translate into individual terms? All too often the results are shattered or unproductive lives or human beings struggling to recover under suspicious glances from co-work-

Internal Revenue Service employees in Massachusetts. Low-income workers who find their jobs tedious and unfulfilling are just as vulnerable to substance abuse as their "fast-track" counterparts.

ers. The following case histories illustrate more than facts and figures ever could about the ruinous consequences, in both personal and professional terms, of runaway substance abuse.

David Perlmutter seemed to have it all. A graduate of Williams College and the New York University Law School, he was an assistant district attorney in New York City assigned to prosecute illicit drug cases. But at some point, Perlmutter crossed the line from prosecutor to criminal. He tried cocaine one day and within three months was addicted to the drug. He soon developed a $1,000 per day habit; what he couldn't afford, he stole, sometimes from evidence gathered for the cases that he was about to prosecute. In 1985 Perlmutter was caught and charged with trafficking in illegal drugs. He received three years in jail and faced the end of his career.

Eliot (not his real name) was a well-paid technical writer for a major computer company. He virtually grew up with alcohol. When he was a teenager he drank at home with his father and went out to bars, where he found that liquor made him less shy with women. He enjoyed the release that cocktails provided, not realizing until too late that he was an alcoholic.

By his mid-thirties, Eliot was drinking more and enjoying it less. Before he went to work, he drank vodka with his coffee. During the day he took frequent nips of liquor. His stomach always felt bad, and he drank to throw up and reduce the pain. His wife was talking about a separation, and the quality of his work was declining. His whole life began to come apart.

Eventually Eliot realized that he needed help to exorcise his personal demon. "I went to work one day, and walked into my supervisor's office, and said, 'I'm an alcoholic and I can't stop drinking. I need some time off to go to a hospital,' " he recounted. "I think I knocked her right off her chair."

George's (not his real name) journey was even more traumatic. The son of an alcoholic father, George started drinking at the age of 14. Two years later, he began to experiment with illicit drugs: marijuana, mescaline, amphetamines, barbiturates, and heroin. However, he generally avoided trouble and after leaving high school joined a branch of a chain store where he eventually became a manager.

George's promotion coincided with the U.S. boom in cocaine, a drug he took to immediately. "I fell in love with it," he recalled. Initially, it seemed a perfect drug. But after six months he began to realize that the drug was dominating his life.

"Cocaine just sneaks up on you," he said. "You can get paid and you can go to the bank and cash your check and say, 'I'm not going to do any tonight.' But all of a sudden, your car just drives itself to the coke dealer's house and your whole paycheck's gone."

As George used increasing amounts of cocaine, his job performance suffered. He began a pattern of arriving late for work on several mornings and occasionally missed entire days. Coincidentally, his supervisors in the store chain noticed shortages in his store's inventory.

"They came up short," he related. "So they put a detective on me. They never caught me stealing, but they saw my night life. Then they confronted me. I didn't steal from them, but I didn't care when I lost my job either. I had enough false confidence that I thought I could get another job." In fact, the next job that George got was as a cook, earning half the $25,000 annual salary that he had received as a store manager.

Finally, after much persuasion from his family and co-workers, George saw how self-destructive his behavior had become. He signed up for a detoxification program, where he learned that he had a "dual dependency" on alcohol and cocaine. Although apparently detoxified, he is aware that he can slip at any time and consequently jeopardize his new job and the relationships he has cultivated since his recovery.

What Can Be Done

Wherever they are discovered, workers who use drugs on the job represent major problems for their employers. According to personnel directors, employees who abuse drugs are more likely to perform poorly, miss work, and lose time while on the job. American industry bears much of the cost of drug use and abuse. According to government estimates, employers lose about $33 billion per year as a result of lost productivity, absenteeism, and increased accident rates directly attributable to drug use. The only industry that profits from drug use is crime: Estimates put the dollar value of illicit drug traffic in the United States as anywhere between $27 and $110 billion annually.

Consequently, employers, increasingly concerned about problems of addiction among their workers, have recognized the need to offer these people something more positive than mere disciplinary action or dismissal. Several companies have encouraged the creation of local chapters of Alcoholics Anonymous and Narcotics Anonymous, organizations that encourage individuals to stay off alcohol or other drugs by offering the strong support of colleagues in the same situation. Other corporations help alcoholics and drug addicts by offering their employees treatment programs and expert counseling on company time.

The *New York Times* reported in March 1987 that the steep rise in numbers of employees with drug problems has, in turn, generated a "mini-industry" of consulting firms designed to help companies cope through the establishment of employee assistance programs. These consulting firms design and monitor EAPs, programs that provide workers with confidential therapy or guide them to outside treatment facilities and resources. In addition, EAPs provide antidrug seminars and literature to workers at a company.

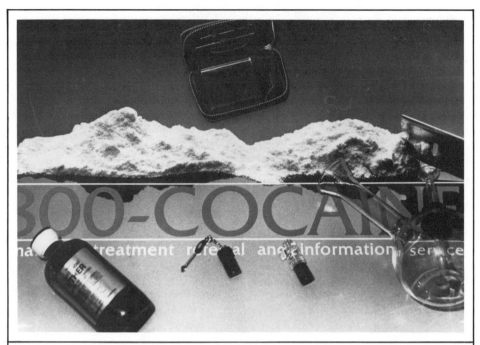

In 1983 Dr. Mark Gold established 1-800-COCAINE, a toll-free cocaine abuse hotline. By that time cocaine had become an extremely popular drug of abuse in professional circles.

Although EAPs have been around since the 1960s to help employees deal with marital or alcohol-related problems, they have only recently begun to focus on helping people with drug problems. Yet in this new area they have already proven to be a valuable ally for firms. The *New York Times* quoted an anonymous source as saying, "We did a study that showed that for every $1 invested in our drug program, we got $7 back in reduced benefits usage and [reduced] absenteeism."

Studies have shown that companies can exert enormous influence on their workers' drug habits. Many addicts are far more likely to seek treatment when faced with the disapproval of their boss than when confronted by their families and friends. "Most people will lose their families before they'll lose their jobs," explained Barbara Feinstein, who runs a company based in Lexington, Massachusetts, that helps employees overcome addictions. Studies by the National Council on Alcoholism and the Conference Board have shown that addicts identified in the workplace and offered treatment programs by their employers have an 80% chance of recovery.

Nonetheless, the road to recovery is difficult. Not only must workers face the mental and physical torment of giving up drug and alcohol addictions, but they must also live with the continuing suspicions of colleagues and supervisors.

According to a lawyer in an East Coast city who was trying to recover from addiction to alcohol and cocaine, a thread of suspicion was sewn among his co-workers and clients. "He's an addict and an alcoholic, and you can't trust him," one client of the lawyer was told. Colleagues in the workplace often consider recovering addicts to be people of weak character, reasoning that, had they been strong enough, the individuals would never have succumbed to the temptation of drugs in the first place.

Supervisors may underestimate the job-related abilities of recovering alcoholics. One woman who worked for a small computer company recalled that after she told her boss she was recovering from addictions to marijuana, amphetamines, and alcohol, the boss took care not to give her difficult assignments and told her co-workers not to put her under stress.

For many on-the-job users of alcohol and drugs, the inevitable sequel to successful treatment is the hunt for a new job. That raises the delicate question of what to tell the potential new employer about the addiction. Generally, recovering addicts find honesty to be the best policy. One insurance executive who underwent treatment after he was fired several times because of his drinking told a job interviewer frankly, "If you don't believe alcoholism is a disease, this is going to be a brief interview." He got the job, but recalled that "I could feel the eyes of that office on me for several months."

Even when on-the-job addicts have passed through treatment with apparent success, they say that they continually must be on guard against their own tendency to return to alcohol or drugs and against the distrust of their fellow workers. The working world does not easily forgive a colleague who has traded in responsibility on the job for seemingly reckless drug use. However, perhaps it is enough that employers finally are attempting to understand the agony and hardships of conquering drug addiction and, in doing so, are willing to help rather than to punish workers as they fight to regain control.

Secretary of Transportation Elizabeth Dole speaks out against drug and alcohol abuse among all workers with responsibility for public safety.

CHAPTER 3

PUBLIC SAFETY AT RISK

Responding to data that revealed an increasing use of drugs by employees on the job, private and public firms across the country began instituting drug-testing procedures for employees in the mid-1980s. This practice quickly became a controversial issue in which questions arose concerning individuals' rights to privacy. Employers contended, however, that workers can be impaired while using drugs on the job and risk hurting themselves and others. Indeed, some drugs can remain in a person's system for days after ingestion and slow down mental or physical abilities for hours after the euphoric effects of the drug have worn off. These facts, advocates of testing say, justify the necessity of drug testing, at least for many workers who are placed in a position of responsibility for public safety while on duty. Even civil libertarians concede that certain jobs in which public safety is involved justify the use of some means of guaranteeing drug-free practitioners.

Unfortunately, studies show that at least small numbers of such employees are not drug-free. Some physicians, air traffic controllers, pilots, police officers, locomotive engineers, technicians in nuclear power stations, and workers in other pursuits critical to public safety are abusing drugs before, after, and during their hours of employment. Drug use by individuals whose actions can put other lives at risk is an alarming prospect.

Because public transportation workers are responsible for the lives of thousands of passengers, drug use among professional drivers, engineers, and pilots is especially dangerous.

Surface Transportation

Consider just one of the trades involving responsibility for human lives: driving public-transportation vehicles, such as buses, passenger trains, and subway cars. In a speech in New York in September 1986, James Burnett, chairman of the National Transportation Safety Board (NTSB) reported, "One-half of all rapid-transit accidents we investigated in the last couple of years have been due to drugs, legal and illicit. We can't prove direct causal effect, but the problem was certainly there."

Burnett's assertion was not entirely accepted. Leaders of transportation workers' unions took issue with the magnitude of the figure, and the NTSB eventually conceded that its numbers were based on anecdotal evidence rather than formal studies. There is little disagreement, however, that some professional drivers do perform their jobs under the influence of drugs that can impair their judgment and their passengers' safety. The Federal Railroad Administration reported that alcohol and drug use played a part in approximately 48 accidents causing 37 deaths, 80 injuries, and $34.4 million in damages between 1975 and 1984. As a routine measure, the Federal Railroad Administration now tests new employees for drug use and also tests current employees whom supervisors suspect of substance abuse.

A particularly disturbing allegation of links between drugs and transport driving occurred in the wake of a fatal rail accident near Baltimore on January 4, 1987. The accident, which killed 16 people, resulted when an Amtrak passenger train slammed into 3 linked Conrail locomotives that had gone through several warning signals and a halt signal. Drug tests showed that the Conrail engineer and brakeman both had marijuana in their systems at the time of the accident, although it remained unclear to what extent, if any, the drug had affected their working ability.

Rescuers survey the wreck of an Amtrak train that collided with a Conrail train in 1987. The Conrail employees responsible for the crash had marijuana in their bloodstream at the time.

As a result of this accident, the National Transportation Safety Board conducted its own investigation into possible reasons for the train collision. However, this investigation has uncovered alleged inconsistencies in the drug tests. In April 1987 the board found that drug tests on the Conrail crew members made by the Civil Aeromedical Institute were at odds with a similar examination of substances in the crew's blood that was made by a University of Utah team.

Even as the railroad industry is acknowledging that occasional drug use on the job is occurring among some railroad workers, it must also contend with the problem that its own methods of drug testing may be inaccurate and need to be reassessed. A consistent antidrug program for railroad workers consequently may still be in the developing stages.

The Friendly Skies?

Airline pilots are another group of professionals who have enormous responsibilities for public safety when they are on duty. While they are off duty, however, alcohol has long been the drug of choice for some. In *The Right Stuff* (1979), an account of the beginning of the United States space program, Tom Wolfe wrote about the small group of test pilots at Edwards Air Force Base in California's remote Mojave desert. Wolfe recounted that "drinking and driving and driving and drinking" were the dominant occupations for these pilots. More recently, a 1986 report by the U.S. Department of Transportation stated that roughly 16,000 individuals who had been convicted of drunken driving between 1960 and 1986 had licenses to fly airplanes. Furthermore, about 7,000 of them had not admitted their convictions during the medical reviews that they were required to take periodically to keep their flying licenses. Exactly how much of a problem these statistics represented to the flying public was questionable. According to officials at the Department of Transportation, only between 1,000 and 2,000 of these convicted individuals flew commercial passenger planes. Furthermore, there is no evidence that someone who will drive drunk will fly a plane under the influence of alcohol. "Just because you drive drunk on the ground, there's no correlation that you're going to fly drunk," said William Daniels, a department official. "But that's an indication that you have a drinking problem."

Author Tom Wolfe at the Kennedy Space Center in Cape Canaveral Florida. His book The Right Stuff, *on the beginnings of the United States space program, chronicled the legendary affinity between pilots and alcohol.*

Even pilots who carefully and faithfully follow the Federal Aviation Administration's rules that forbid them to fly less than eight hours after consuming alcohol may have a problem, however. Research reported in the December 1986 issue of the *American Journal of Psychiatry* indicates that a pilot's flying ability may still be impaired 14 hours after his or her last drink — several hours after all detectable evidence of alcohol has left the blood. The studies, by Otto Von Leirer and Jerome Yesavage of Stanford University Medical Center, involved 10 Navy pilots who flew in simulators several hours after drinking enough to make them legally drunk. The pilots failed to follow the standard procedures for takeoffs or landings and missed the correct descent angle in their landings. Generally, Leirer commented, pilots are "very responsible. If they know they're impaired, they'll act accordingly. It's when people are impaired and they don't realize it that you might really have a big problem."

The Federal Aviation Agency, the Airline Medical Department, and the Airline Pilots Association had the insight to recognize alcoholism as a problem among pilots in 1973. At that time, these three groups set up an alcohol rehabilitation program for pilots and persuaded professionals to volunteer for treatment if necessary. Eight years later, the program was able to report that at least three hundred pilots had sought help to cope with their addiction.

No commercial airline accident has ever been attributed to drug use, and the few studies that have been undertaken suggest that drug abuse by pilots is rare; a 1985 survey, for example, showed that less than 1% of American Airlines's 9,000 pilots used drugs. Drugs have been implicated, however, in flight deaths among private pilots, who have obvious responsibilities in regard to other planes and passengers, as well as to people living beneath the airspace in which they travel. Federal Aviation Administration (FAA) figures indicate

Air traffic controllers test a collision alert system. Public safety demands that these highly stressed workers remain drug and alcohol free while on duty.

the presence of illegal drugs in the blood of 0.05% of pilots killed in crashes, and of alcohol in 7.5%. The National Transportation Safety Board (NTSB) noted 10 drug-related fatal air accidents in 1983 and 1984, which killed more than 30 people overall. A report from Pittsburgh, Pennsylvania, in the summer of 1986 showed that area hospitals had treated at least 23 cases of drug abuse by flight crew members over a matter of months. Twenty of the cases involved cocaine, two heroin, and the other, Valium and alcohol.

The FAA became concerned enough in 1986 to consider random drug tests for flight crews. "Drug and alcohol abuse [is] a major problem in society," stated an FAA report. "The FAA does not have any conclusive information that drug and alcohol abuse among personnel engaged in aviation activities is any lesser or greater than that of the general public."

Yet, it is also true that pilots who use mind-altering substances are putting many more people at risk than a sales clerk or an executive who abuses drugs. "Where the safe transportation of the public is concerned, there can be no tolerance for drug or alcohol abuse," declared Secretary of Transportation Elizabeth Dole.

Air Traffic Control

A pilot is responsible for the safety of a few hundred passengers at most. An air traffic controller bears the load for several planes carrying many hundreds of people altogether. This harassed profession has been the target of several accusations of drug use. At a Lancaster, California, center that handles 1.6 million planes per year, 3 of 140 air traffic controllers were taken off their jobs in August 1986 after authorities received proof that they had used cocaine, amphetamines, and marijuana in their off-duty hours. During the months following that incident, five controllers in the Kansas City Air Traffic Control Center were removed from duty for the same reason, and a Florida controller was arrested after cocaine was found in a package mailed to him. The pressures of this job may, in fact, induce controllers to turn to drugs for relief. But there can be few excuses for the controller working under the influence of drugs when the potential for tragedy and loss of lives as a result of human error at such jobs is so great.

Nuclear Power Plants

The safety of nuclear power in the United States has been a matter of considerable controversy since 1979, when the Three Mile Island plant in Pennsylvania suffered a major accident that released some radiation into the atmosphere. The disaster at the Soviet Union's Chernobyl plant in April 1986, which killed about a dozen people and injured hundreds of others, intensified the debate. If a nuclear power plant should for any reason malfunction, it could threaten thousands of people with death, injury, or illness from radiation and contaminate the region surrounding it for hundreds of years.

Defenders of nuclear power contend that the United States' plants have safety features that will stop any runaway nuclear reaction before it releases dangerous amounts of radioactivity into the environment. Opponents counter that, although the machines may be reliable, there is always a chance of human error that could lead to tragedy on a vast scale.

Against this background, reports surfaced in 1986 that workers in at least two U.S. nuclear power plants were abusing drugs and alcohol. Police, physicians, local prosecutors, and former construction workers at the controversial Seabrook nuclear power plant in New Hampshire contended that members of construction crews building the plant often used drugs and alcohol on the job. In another case, officials in the state of Washington withdrew security clearances from 69 employees at the federal government's Hanover nuclear reservation, the site of several working nuclear reactors, because of alleged drug abuses in 1985 and 1986.

For local residents concerned about the safety of the completed Seabrook plant (which has yet to start generating electricity), the charges of drug and alcohol abuse by its builders were particularly frightening. Reports that construction workers were arrested for drunken driving on the way to and from work at the site, revelations that drugs were used at the plant, and stories of parties featuring drugs and alcohol occurring on the plant's grounds made even supporters of nuclear power suspicious of the plant's safety.

Initial charges came from opponents of the plant, who were gathering evidence to forestall Seabrook's operation. Seabrook's owners denied widespread abuse of alcohol and drugs by their employees, but they did admit that they had

The completed Seabrook nuclear power plant. Some builders working on the plant had a long record of drug and alcohol abuse on the job.

fired 289 workers from the project between 1976 and 1986 for use of these substances.

The *Boston Globe* added fuel to this argument, quoting Dr. Sylvia Kennedy, a physician in the emergency room of Exeter Hospital, on the death by acute alcohol intoxication of a worker taken to that hospital directly from the Seabrook plant in 1981. The incident "crystallized a lot of other things I had seen in the emergency room," said Kennedy. "That was the point at which I said, 'Hey, wait a minute, these people are building a nuclear plant.' Could this plant have safe workmanship if this type of alcohol abuse was going on?"

The Men and Women in Blue

If a nuclear power plant employee who becomes involved with drugs threatens public safety, police officers who do the same can destroy public trust. Over the years, some officers in large cities have accepted protection money from drug pushers; others have extorted money from such individuals or have confiscated drugs, which they then sell. A few police officers have gone one step further, becoming addicts themselves, at the mercy of the pushers they should be pursuing. High-ranking members of some city police departments fear that such drug dependence is growing as young officers from environments in which drug use is widely accepted join police departments.

According to one officer who had to leave his job and enter a center for drug treatment, the typical pattern starts when an individual habitually uses drugs in secondary school and college. After observing a period of abstinence at police college, where random drug tests are performed, the officer often joins a police department in a large city. There, the rookie finds fellow officers who use marijuana, cocaine, and other drugs during off-duty hours. With his new peers or

Graduates of the New York City Police Academy stand at attention. Police officers who take illicit drugs destroy public trust and abuse their tremendous responsibility to maintain law and order.

alone, the young officer returns to old drug habits. He or she learns to trust a "code of silence" among other officers that persists even when they might suspect that someone on the force is using drugs. As the officer becomes more dependent on drugs, he or she starts arriving late for work and begins to care less about the job. Yet the officer is afraid to admit to a drug habit, because it is cause for immediate dismissal. He or she remains on the job for as long as possible, unwilling to seek help.

The possibility that some police officers were using drugs led departments and law enforcement officials in cities across the nation to recommend drug tests for employees. In April 1986 the *New York Times* ran a story saying that police in Boston would be undergoing drug tests. On the heels of that announcement, New Jersey attorney general W. Cary Edwards urged in October that applicants, trainees, and law-enforcement officers who carried firearms in the state submit to drug tests. Positive testing would lead to dismissal. Edward's office estimated that fewer than 2% of the 30,000 people tested actually used illegal drugs; still, it was a matter of concern.

Physician Heal Thyself

Doctors are, perhaps, the professionals with the easiest access to drugs. They are devoted to using drugs to heal patients. But they can also fall victim to the temptation to "prescribe" drugs for themselves. Occasional use can lead to dependency on stimulants to relieve fatigue and tranquilizers to alleviate stress; unknowingly, the doctor can become the addict. Instead of undergoing treatment for their condition, they may continue to practice medicine while seriously impaired in their judgment and performance.

According to David Smith, director of the Haight-Ashbury Free Medical Clinic in San Francisco, physicians' rate of addiction to prescribed narcotics is four to six times higher than that of the general public. A team at the Harvard School of Public Health reported in the *New England Journal of Medicine* that 10% of a group of 500 practicing physicians regularly used drugs and that 3% were addicted. Several of the users treated themselves with drugs available in hospital pharmacies, instead of taking the drugs at home for recreational use.

47

As far back as 1979, this situation was being discussed in medical circles. According to the book *Confessions of a Medical Heretic* (1979), by Dr. Robert S. Mendelsohn, "Conservative counts peg ... the number of alcoholic [doctors in the United States] at more than 30,000 and the number of narcotic addicts at 3,500 or one percent. ... Even the American Medical Association admits that one and a half percent of doctors in the United States abuse drugs."

Doctors are not the only medical professionals to fall under the spell of addiction. Nurses and pharmacists, both of whom have easy access to drugs, have been identified as high risk candidates for drug abuse. In fact, the problem of substance abuse in the nursing profession has reached such proportions that numerous treatment programs designed specifically to help these troubled men and women have appeared around the country. An article in the *New York Times* in July 1986 described the extent of dependency among nurses. The newspaper quoted Dr. Madeline Naegle, chairperson of the American Nursing Association's Committee on Impaired Nursing Practice, as stating that between 5 and 6%, or 100,000, of 1.9 million registered nurses in the United States abuse drugs. They obtain substances at the hospitals by diverting supplies, forging signatures for stockroom orders, filling prescriptions that have been terminated, or by giving patients placebos instead of their required medications.

A nationwide law passed in recognition of this problem requires hospitals to report cases of drug abuse among nurses to their state's board of nursing. A nurse must appear before a panel that hears his or her account of the problem. The nurse is then often put on probation and ordered to submit to random drug tests, or his or her license is suspended while he or she receives substance abuse counseling. Under certain circumstances, a nurse's license may be revoked.

Anesthesiologists, who administer a variety of drugs to patients to induce unconsciousness before major surgery, suffer most from easy access to drugs. Their rate of addiction is high enough to qualify it as an occupational hazard, according to one expert. A synthetic anesthetic known as fentanyl is one of the most powerful and dangerous drugs used by this group. The substance is 100 times as strong as morphine and much more addictive than cocaine.

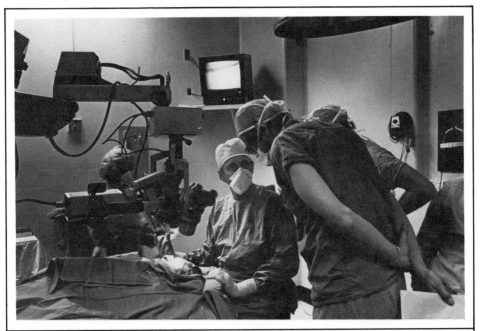

Doctors with drug habits often fail to acknowledge the problem until they are seriously at risk. Because they have such easy access to drugs, their addictions can remain secret for years.

Physicians who abuse drugs do not necessarily reveal their problem through slips or lapses in their work habits. According to Dr. Will Spiegelman, a specialist on addiction at Stanford University Hospital, doctors typically do not begin functioning poorly until two or more years after they are addicted. By this time, they are in deep trouble.

It is equally difficult to predict which doctors are most vulnerable to drug abuse. One study suggests that individuals who have psychological difficulties before they attend medical school are more likely than others to abuse drugs and alcohol in the course of their professional lives. It is also possible that drug problems in the individual's family foreshadow abuse. As the medical profession seeks to cut down on drug abuse by its members, by urging therapeutic counseling or insisting on suspension of duties for the addict, it has little more than speculation to work with when identifying the physicians most at risk.

A meeting of Alcoholics Anonymous. A specialized, international program, Doctors in AA follows principles of mutual support for physicians attempting to overcome drinking problems.

Helping the Health Care Professionals

Once addiction has set in, early detection and intervention have been identified as the most effective ways to cut down on the incidence of drug abuse among health care professionals. There are a number of steps that can be taken to treat them. Access to drugs can and should be limited. A medical professional's involvement in dispensing medication may be curtailed; narcotics licenses may be revoked; sometimes a career change is necessary.

The psychological treatment of addicted health care professionals is somewhat specialized, largely because these users often minimize the severity of their problem and rationalize their reasons for using drugs. In addition, they frequently express the belief that they are different from other addicts and therefore do not require treatment. They are extremely frightened of being discovered, and so will go to great lengths to cover up their addiction. They also seek to control their own treatment and resist getting help from others.

Specialized treatment programs and self-help groups have emerged to deal with these problems. The international

Doctors in AA is, perhaps, the best known of the self-help groups for professionals. It follows principles of mutual support in the interests of maintaining sobriety and encourages its members to participate in traditional treatment programs.

Do the stressful jobs of pilots, police, and physicians make these individuals more vulnerable to the temptations of drugs and alcohol? The common assumption is that people who undergo mental stress in the workplace tend to use drugs in order to unwind. At least one expert disagrees with that point of view. "It's not the job, it's not the atmosphere," explained Dr. Stanley Mohler of Wright State University in Dayton, Ohio. "It's the individual who needs a chemical for a euphoric feeling. You can put certain people in any job and they'd have the same problem until they got help."

The plight of college basketball star Len Bias, who died of cocaine poisoning days after this picture was taken, focused national attention on the issue of drug abuse among sports stars.

CHAPTER 4

THE BIG STARS

Magnetized by the allure of society's stars, pill peddlers — whether they be solicitous doctors, illicit drug dealers, sycophantic "friends," or mere hangers-on—often seek to curry favor with the rich and famous. Top athletes, successful actors, and popular musicians have the kind of money it takes to finance a serious involvement with drugs. The circles that celebrities travel in are rife with those who quite discreetly provide drugs. In a milieu saturated with drugs and alcohol, big money, easy sex, enormous pressure, and fragile but gigantic egos, the ground for chemical dependency is fertile. Many celebrities engage in casual "recreational" use of drugs and alcohol; others use these substances in an effort to manage the anxiety and stress of their fast-track lives. Eventually, however, the long-term consequences of this involvement with drugs lead to addictions, ruined careers, and even death for many of its victims.

The World of Sports

No event alerted the public to the nation's drug problem more strikingly than the death of Len Bias on June 19, 1986. A star basketball player at the University of Maryland, Bias represented the essence of college athletic success. Two days before he died he had been selected as the second player in

This vase painting showing runners in the original Olympic Games dates from the 6th century B.C.E. According to one researcher, athletes at some early Olympics used drugs.

the National Basketball Association's draft by the 1986 world champions, the Boston Celtics. Bias's ability on the court and his likable personality seemed to guarantee a brilliant professional career.

Bias celebrated his NBA selection with friends on the night of June 18 at a party that featured cocaine. Early the following morning, Bias had a bad reaction to the drug and was rushed to the hospital. He never recovered.

A week later, the American sports world was shaken by the drug-induced death of yet another young athlete. Don Rogers, a 23-year-old defensive back with the National Football League's Cleveland Browns, was to be married on June 28, 1986. He celebrated his impending nuptials with a few friends the evening before. Like Bias, he used cocaine. And like Bias, he did not survive the party.

These two cases of drug use among athletes are, unfortunately, not an aberration. Research by John Toner of the University of Connecticut reveals that drug use was a problem among the stars of the original Olympic Games as far back as 700 B.C.E. (B.C.E. means Before the Common Era, the same period as B.C.) According to Toner, the games were suspended for 17 years because of substance abuse. Toner speculated that some drug derived from the coca leaf was used by athletes even then.

In modern times, despite harsh regulations and penalties, drug use continues to be a recreational, medicinal, or therapeutic activity among many of the finest professionals in a wide range of sports. In some of the most popular American sports — baseball, football, and basketball — there is evidence that illicit drugs are available to, and often abused by, athletes.

Major League Baseball

During much of 1985, baseball fans focused almost as much attention on a courtroom in Pittsburgh, Pennsylvania, as on their teams' exploits on the diamond. The reason for this fixation was a long-running trial in which drug dealers were accused of supplying a lineup of well-known players with cocaine and other recreational drugs. The case, during which a number of players called as witnesses admitted to using illicit drugs, infuriated baseball authorities and threatened to tarnish the "all-American" image fans had of their favorite players and teams.

"Baseball is the American game," said Boston Red Sox general manager Lou Gorman. "Kids look up with tremendous admiration at these guys as role models, and it's only natural that they begin thinking, 'Hey, if players take drugs, then maybe drugs are OK.' "

In light of revelations emerging at the Pittsburgh trial, baseball commissioner Peter Ueberroth imposed harsh financial penalties on players implicated in drug use at the trial. At the same time, he indicated that if these athletes wanted to continue playing on a professional team, they would have to submit to periodic testing to detect drug use. Ueberroth also attempted to impose urine testing for drug use on *all* players on professional teams, but he was was blocked in this effort by the Major League Baseball Players Association. Currently, there is no official agreement on the issue of drug testing among baseball players; negotiations on the issue are expected in 1988.

Football and Basketball

Needless to say, no major sport has a monopoly on drug use. In professional football, Tony Elliott of the New Orleans Saints went through thousands of dollars and sold his furniture, his car, and his wife's wedding ring in order to buy drugs. He decided to seek treatment, he recalled, only when, in an effort to hold up a drug dealer, he found himself at the wrong end of the dealer's .357 Magnum. The family of running back Warren McVea refused to bail him out of jail on charges of cocaine possession until he could be admitted directly into a treatment center. Tight end Clarence Kay of the Denver Broncos considered himself lucky to play in the 1987 Super Bowl against the New York Giants in Pasadena; he had been suspended for four weeks late in the regular season after a urine test revealed he had been using drugs.

Recognizing that drug use among NFL players does occur and could conceivably impinge on the overall strength of team playing, the NFL Players Association and team owners adopted drug-testing procedures in 1982 calling for mandatory drug tests of all players before the start of the season. If a player tests positive for drugs or if the team doctor suspects that an athlete is using drugs, that player may be subjected to additional tests during the season and/or drug counseling.

In the early 1980s, professional basketball appeared to have the worst drug problems among its players. However, the National Basketball Association went on to establish a strict drug-testing policy for its members, one of the most successful such antidrug policies in professional sports. Instituted in 1983, the National Basketball Association's plan gives a player two chances to volunteer that he has used drugs and then to receive rehabilitative treatment. It also requires players suspected of illicit drug use to submit to urinalysis. If the player fails the test, he is banned from the league for life, although he can apply for reinstatement after two years. "The whole idea of the program is to get you to come forward voluntarily," said Larry Fleischer of the NBA Players Association. "If you don't, you bear the burden."

To judge from the record, that burden is heavy indeed. Several players were found to be using illegal drugs, particularly cocaine, in the program's early years, and some con-

The family of football player Warren McVea refused to bail him out of jail on charges of cocaine possession until he could be admitted directly into a treatment center.

tinued to do so even when they knew that discovery of their ongoing habit would destroy their professional careers. John Drew of the Atlanta Hawks was the first player to be banned from the NBA, when he checked into a drug treatment program for the third time, in 1986. Michael Ray Richardson, a supremely talented guard with the New Jersey Nets, was also banned after a urinalysis following his second attempt at drug rehabilitation. In January 1987 Lewis Lloyd and Mitchell Wiggins, who had helped the Houston Rockets reach the NBA finals the previous season, were both banned from the league after testing positive for cocaine.

Ralph Sampson, their teammate on the Rockets, described the pressure under which many top athletes must live. "Sooner or later, we all have to face the fact that we're targets," said Sampson. "There's women, there's drug people. It's getting so that you can't say hello to Joe Blow when he yells at you on the street, because you don't know who he is and you have to watch who you are associated with."

The Entertainers

Stars of the stage, television, movies, or music industry are also vulnerable and apt to experiment with drugs, despite threats of bad publicity in the media and obvious consequences to their health and appearance. Entertainment celebrities, graced with money and surrounded by hangers-on, frequently have been involved in drug use, whether out of need or simply for "kicks." The entertainment community is littered with celebrities who have paid a tragic price for their drug and alcohol involvements.

In the early 1980s, John Belushi was, perhaps, the most prominent victim of Hollywood's love affair with drugs. Belushi, the crazed class clown in the movie *Animal House* (1978) and star of the long-running television show "Saturday Night Live," short-circuited his own swift rise to fame with numerous instances of drug abuse that, for the most part, were covered up by television executives, family, and friends. On March 5, 1982, his addictions could no longer be hidden from the public. That day, Belushi was found dead of a drug overdose, a result of combining heroin with cocaine. The deadly injection had been given to him by a "friend," Catherine Smith. Smith was later brought to trial for her involvement in Belushi's death.

Comedian Richard Pryor had a brush with catastrophe in the early 1980s, when he sustained near-fatal burns apparently while trying to free-base cocaine. Pryor recovered and a few years later produced and performed in a film, *Jo Jo Dancer, Your Life Is Calling*, that candidly addressed the hazards of involvement with the drug culture.

Boy George, the flamboyant British pop singer, has also had serious drug problems. Two of his close friends died from overdoses of heroin and methadone in the same year that he was being treated for heroin addiction in England.

Heroin, cocaine, and other illegal drugs are not the only substances abused by celebrities. Many entertainers misuse alcohol and a wide variety of prescription drugs as well, and talent is no protection against these problems. The list of patients who have sought treatment for various addictions during the 1980s reads like a *Who's Who* of the entertainment world; it includes Elizabeth Taylor, Liza Minnelli, Robert Mitchum, Tony Curtis, Johnny Cash, Mary Tyler Moore, and Chevy Chase.

Of course, stars are not the only people in the entertainment industry using and abusing drugs. Many people behind the scenes, including set designers, stunt people, directors, and producers are notorious drug abusers. A current NIDA survey of employees in the entertainment or recreation industries indicated that approximately 17% of people in these industries use marijuana during working hours. Approximately 27% use cocaine on the job.

In efforts to help members of their own ranks, major studios, television networks, unions, and various organizations affiliated with entertainment came together in 1984 to form an industrywide employee assistance program (EAP) for drug abusers in the industry. Dubbed the Entertainment Industry Referral and Assistance Center (EIRAC), this program currently receives approximately 40 calls each month from employers or employees looking for help.

Rock star Boy George leaving the court where he was fined for heroin possession in 1986. The relentless pressures of the entertainment business have driven many stars to drug abuse.

Actress and film star Elizabeth Taylor is one of many stars who underwent treatment for drug dependency during the 1980s.

Broadcasting the Problem

Over the past few years, many people have accused the entertainment industry of either indirectly or directly communicating its own casual attitudes toward drug usage to the general public via movies, television shows, and songs that condone, even celebrate, experimentation. In 1969, the movie *Easy Rider* sympathetically depicted a character played by Peter Fonda as a habitual user of marijuana. Casual use of drugs was portrayed as an accepted practice in many subsequent movies, among them *Annie Hall*, *Midnight Express*, *The Big Chill*, and *Desperately Seeking Susan*.

In fact, such portrayals have outraged many antidrug crusaders who are associated with the entertainment industry. "Why did little kids go to see *Desperately Seeking Susan?*" asked Susan Newman, daughter of actor Paul Newman and sister of the late Scott Newman, who died from an overdose of Valium and alcohol. "Because of [rock star] Madonna. And what did they see Madonna doing throughout the movie? Smoking marijuana."

In the wake of Scott's tragic death, the Newman family in 1981 set up a center designed to educate the public about the hazards and consequences of drug abuse. Other members of the entertainment industry are also trying to recruit their peers in a war against drugs. A number of media professionals came together in the 1980s to form the Entertainment Industries Council (EIC). EIC is currently working to recruit members of the entertainment industry to participate in antidrug publicity campaigns across the country. Groups such as NIDA and the National Association of Broadcasters Task Force have also stepped up campaigns to encourage celebrities to speak out against drugs.

Obviously, drug abuse problems still exist among the exclusive circles of people producing much of the entertainment for the nation. But growing numbers of influential people in that area are also taking a responsible look at both their own actions and the influence they have over a vast audience on this complex issue.

Women in the 1980s have more opportunities than ever in such previously male-dominated fields as business and law, but they must deal with unprecedented conflicts between family and career.

CHAPTER 5

WOMEN AND DRUGS

Women in American society won many battles for economic, social, and political equality during the 1970s and 1980s. Their rights to employment and respect in formerly male-dominated areas — the operating room, the boardroom, the police force, and the armed forces — were secured not only in a series of legislative victories, but in changing public perceptions of "woman's place" as well.

Not surprisingly, however, women's changing roles have brought with them a complex of new anxieties and stresses and a rising incidence among women of the chronic companion of anxiety and stress — substance abuse. Several studies indicate that almost half of the 10 to 13 million alcoholics in the United States are female, although alcoholism traditionally has been regarded as a disease that victimized men almost exclusively. The rate of smoking among women is on the rise, as is the use of cocaine.

However, one of the major causes of substance abuse among women is iatrogenic. (Iatrogenic describes health problems that arise specifically from unsound medical practice.) In some cases, female patients being treated by doctors become addicted to the drugs prescribed for them. In other cases, doctors will prescribe unwisely, sometimes by failing to monitor their patients closely enough and continuing medication past the point where its use is medically warranted.

According to a 1978 report published by NIDA, during the previous year 36 million American women had used tranquilizers, 16 million women had used sleeping pills, and 12 million had used stimulants, mostly in the form of diet pills. For a number of decades until the early 1980s, about 90% of women treated in hospital emergency rooms for drug-related problems had used prescription drugs, often in combination with alcohol.

In their 1982 book, *Women Under Stress*, Donald Ray Morse, D.D.S. and M. Lawrence Furst, Ph.D. confirmed the high rate of prescription drug use among women. According to Morse and Furst, more than 2 million women were identified as drug users in the United States in the early 1980s. As a group, these users were by and large addicted to major tranquilizers such as Thorazine, antianxiety agents such as Valium, barbiturates such as Nembutal, antidepressants such as Elavil, and amphetamines such as Dexedrine. Men were by and large the major abusers of such illegal drugs as marijuana, cocaine, and heroin. In *Managing the Drugs in Your Life* (1983), Stephen Levy, Ph.D. pointed out that a House Select Committee on Narcotics Abuse and Control investigating drug use among women came to the following conclusions: 32 million females compared to 19 million males used tranquilizers prescribed by a doctor; 16 million women used prescription sedatives as compared to 12 million men.

Facing the Facts

The problem of drug abuse among women was almost invisible to the nation at large until 1977. Then Betty Ford, whose husband Gerald had just lost the presidency to Jimmy Carter, publicly admitted that she was seeking treatment for addiction to alcohol and prescription drugs. The initial shock created by this announcement soon gave way to a realization that Betty Ford's situation was hardly aberrant. Women in positions far less exalted than hers recognized their own ordeals or those of friends in Mrs. Ford's candid and harrowing revelations. Her honesty and courage enabled thousands of women to confront and reconsider the possibility that they, too, were addicted to pills and/or alcohol.

In 1977 Betty Ford publically admitted her addiction to pills and alcohol. She went on to conquer these problems and became a role model for thousands of women in similar situations.

Betty Ford continued to address the problem in a positive way. In 1982 she founded the Betty Ford Drug Rehabilitation Center, as part of the Eisenhower Medical Center at Rancho Mirage, California. Most of the 5,000 patients that the center admitted during its first 4 years of operation were people stricken by addiction to drugs, particularly legally prescribed medications.

Why do prescription drugs cause such problems among women? And why are patients not warned by their doctors of the potential for abuse? Studies in recent years of the prescribing habits of doctors and the reactions of their patients suggest some clues.

In her book *The Female Fix* (1980), Muriel Nellis, an expert on the drug-related problems of women, highlights some facts about the relationships among physicians, women, and prescription drugs. More women than men undergo psychological treatment for mental health problems and frequently, prescription drugs are seen by women and their doctors alike as cure-alls for psychological woes. Moreover, women are typically prescribed more than twice the dosage of drugs as men for similar psychological symptoms. Women under stress also tend to do their own prescribing. According to government studies, a large proportion of women who turn up at their doctors' offices for the first time with emotional stress have already tried to treat themselves using alcohol or illicit mood-altering drugs.

Surveys of prescription drug use suggest that women unwittingly abuse their chemical treatments, reasoning that two tranquilizers will be twice as effective as one, without thinking of the consequences of taking more than the prescribed dose. Valium, for example, one of the most widely prescribed drugs in America, has its own aftereffects. According to David Smith of San Francisco's Haight-Ashbury Clinic, it can cause withdrawal symptoms in patients who try to stop taking the drug after using it in only small doses over a period of more than one year. One user for whom Valium was prescribed when the demands of bringing up a young family caused her to feel continually on edge recalled her reaction when she finally decided to give up the drug. "I was miserable," she related. "My nerves were shot, and I felt like I had a virus — exhausted, then aching, then tense. It took between two and three months before I felt normal."

Tranquilizers represent just one prescription route to unintentional drug addiction. Another involves "pep-pills" — forms of amphetamine or related substances. Some of these drugs are designed to boost an individual when he or she is feeling tired in the middle of the day; others have frequently been used to control the appetites of people who want to stay slim or lose a few extra pounds without spending time on exercise or struggling to maintain strict diets.

The Superwoman Syndrome

The effects of prescription drug abuse can be devastating, particularly on a modern career woman who feels that she can only cope with the demands of fulfilling her own job satisfactorily, carry out social requirements attached to her own and her husband's jobs, and bring up a family by continuing to consume pills.

A Los Angeles woman who returned to work after several years as a full-time mother provides a cautionary example. Soon after she started her job in an advertising agency, Eleanor found that she was dozing off during afternoon meetings. She went to her doctor, who prescribed small doses of amphetamine for her. The pills gave her the energy to function during the late afternoons and early evenings, but Eleanor found herself still wide awake at night. So she returned to her doctor, who prescribed a sedative to help her sleep.

The regimen worked — after a fashion. Eleanor was able to control her moods and energy level, but only by taking the pills with increasing regularity. Waking up in a blur, she swallowed an amphetamine. Feeling too wound up to sleep at night, she took a tranquilizer. During the day she had an occasional drink to dampen some of the effects of the amphetamine.

Many women find their new roles in the work world extremely rewarding. Unfortunately, others deal less successfully with stress, which may account for the rising rate of alcoholism among career women.

Eventually, the inevitable happened. Eleanor collapsed after taking a sleeping pill one evening. When she awoke in the hospital emergency room, she confronted the truth. She had been living in a self-induced chemical fog for several months.

Reforms in the Treatment of Women

Fortunately, health care professionals and their female patients are beginning to develop a more cautious attitude toward the use of potentially addictive medications. Nowhere is this new approach more in evidence than in the treatment of pain.

As the study of physical pain and its causes has become an increasingly important area in specialized medicine, practitioners of pain therapy are introducing drug-free techniques to help patients deal with chronic aches and pains. Biofeedback (an electronically controlled method that teaches an

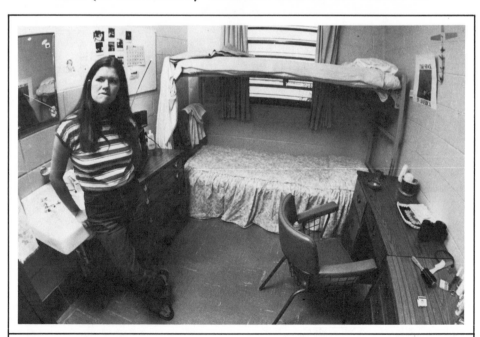

A woman imprisoned for stealing to support her drug habit. Reforms in many states mandate that drug addicts, both male and female, charged with criminal acts be sent to treatment centers rather than prisons.

individual to monitor and modify bodily functions), auto-genic training (a practice involving learning mental exercises that generate a state of relaxation), meditation, hypnosis, and acupuncture are just some of the methods that have won acceptance among physicians in the past decade.

Another positive development in the years following the foundation of the Betty Ford treatment facility is that drug-treatment centers of all types increasingly cater to female patients. Women who want help to overcome their addic-tions — to prescribed or unprescribed, legal or illegal drugs — can find treatment centers just as easily as their male coun-terparts. Weight-reduction clinics emphasizing the combi-nation of properly selected diet and exercise, rather than amphetamines, as the best way to shed pounds and keep them off are also growing in popularity among both males and females in the 1980s.

These developments should ensure that times and atti-tudes have changed enough to guarantee that a situation that existed in Massachusetts until quite recently will never repeat itself. Until the end of 1986, courts in Massachusetts sent women whom they deemed to require treatment for alco-holism to jail, where they often spent more than 20 hours a day locked in their cells. Male alcoholics did not receive such sentences; instead, they were provided treatment through a state addiction center, located in a state hospital. Only when the *Boston Globe* brought the matter to their attention did Massachusetts authorities move quickly to alter the routine jailing of female alcoholics. Only then did the state's secretary of human services announce that he had halted the practice and directed that the women receive the same therapy in treatment centers as men.

A marijuana "smoke-in" on a college campus in 1977. Use of marijuana by college students has declined slightly since the early 1970s but it is still commonplace on most campuses.

CHAPTER 6

YOUNG PEOPLE TURNING ON, TUNING OUT

The increase in drug use and abuse that started in the 1960s matched an increase in the number of teenagers in the United States population. To many authorities, that was no coincidence. Drug use of some sort, whether involving alcohol, marijuana, or harder drugs, became almost a rite of passage for many high school and college students in the 1960s and 1970s. Recent reports show that drugs, especially alcohol, still play a very important role in the social lives of American teenagers. According to a 1986 study in Los Angeles, more than half that city's students had tried drugs by the time they reached the 11th grade.

The Ivory Tower

In the 1980s, drug use can be found to be a pervasive practice among students of virtually all ages, despite massive media, political, and legal campaigns to eliminate drugs from the school environment. On college campuses, the situation has not changed much since the 1960s, a period when substance experimentation among college students became routine. According to a study done by the University of Michigan's Institute for Social Research in 1986, about 30% of students enrolled in college at that time expected to use cocaine at least once before they graduated. The college crowd found no difficulty in obtaining the drug, and until shortly before the survey was taken, most students had perceived little risk in experimenting with cocaine.

Additional facts in the survey showed that college students were following the rest of the population in its tendency to abuse drugs. Among college students, use of such illegal substances as marijuana and amphetamines declined somewhat between 1980 and 1984 and appeared to have stabilized at a level much lower than that of the 1970s. But drug use in general remained a problem in colleges across the country. One undergraduate quoted in the Harvard University newspaper *The Crimson* boasted that Harvard was "the ideal drug environment." The newspaper estimated that as many as 100 undergraduates were involved in drug-dealing.

In addition to using illegal drugs, college students continue to abuse their bodies with alcohol, a perennial and potentially dangerous drug of abuse. Recognizing this fact, Yale University organized a campuswide information campaign about the dangers of alcohol in 1986, after a sophomore died as an apparent result of heavy drinking. One component of the campaign was the appointment of a full-time alcohol counselor.

U.S. secretary of education William J. Bennett launched a publicity campaign in 1986 designed to force college presidents to take drug use on campus more seriously. In many colleges, Bennett complained, "Drug use is open and the institutions have acquiesced in the problem. They don't seem to go to a great deal of trouble to stop it."

Many college authorities expressed their violent disagreement with that thesis. While admitting that drugs and drug dealers were present on their campuses, they argued that they and their administrations were making inroads against the drug culture. Harvard, for example, expelled several students in the early 1980s for drug-related offenses.

Secondary Schools

According to data compiled by NIDA on drug use in schools, students are acquainted with and use a great variety of licit and illicit drugs by the time they graduate from high school.

Drug Usage: America's High School Students (By Percent)									
Type of Drug	Class of 1975	Class of 1976	Class of 1977	Class of 1978	Class of 1979	Class of 1980	Class of 1981	Class of 1982	Class of 1983	Class of 1984
Marijuana/Hashish	47.3	52.8	56.4	59.2	60.4	60.3	59.5	58.7	57.0	54.9
Inhalants	NA	10.3	11.1	12.0	12.7	11.9	12.3	12.8	13.6	14.4
Hallucinogens	16.3	15.1	13.9	14.3	14.1	13.3	13.3	12.5	11.9	10.7
Cocaine	9.0	9.7	10.8	12.9	15.4	15.7	16.5	16.0	16.2	16.1
Heroin	2.2	1.8	1.8	1.6	1.1	1.1	1.1	1.2	1.2	1.3
Stimulants	22.3	22.6	23.0	22.9	24.2	26.4	32.2	35.6	35.4	NA
Sedatives	18.2	17.7	17.4	16.0	14.6	14.9	16.0	15.2	14.4	13.3
Tranquilizers	17.0	16.8	18.0	17.0	16.3	15.2	14.7	14.0	13.3	12.4
Alcohol	90.4	91.9	92.5	93.1	93.0	93.2	92.6	92.8	92.6	92.6
Cigarettes	73.6	75.4	75.7	75.3	74.0	71.0	71.0	70.1	70.6	69.7

Table 2

Source: National Institute on Drug Abuse/Univ. of Michigan Institute for Social Research

Results are based on large, representative sample surveys of the last ten graduating classes enrolled in public and private high schools across the United States.

Results of this study were compiled from sample surveys of 10 graduating classes enrolled in both public and private high schools across the United States from 1975 to 1984. As indicated in Table 2, use by high school students of alcohol, cigarettes, and marijuana was consistently high between 1975 and 1984. Though comparatively lower, the rising instance of cocaine use among high school students is also notable. Use of prescription stimulants and depressants, especially because these figures reflect only drug use that was not under a doctor's orders, is another cause for concern. America's high school students are experimenting with a broad spectrum of drugs, and there is no evidence that this potentially dangerous experimentation is on the wane.

In the 1980s drug use among teenagers implies a different set of circumstances than it did 10 or 20 years ago. One difference is that alcohol has again become the drug of choice for adolescents, as it was in the 1950s. And the experiences of teenagers who started or continued to use illicit drugs in the 1980s were rather different from what their parents' generation experienced in the 1960s. First, as has been noted, there was the rapid increase in cocaine use and availability. Second, even students who restricted themselves to marijuana were smoking something stronger than their parents had. Studies by the University of Mississippi for NIDA showed that the average proportion of the active ingredient in marijuana, THC, increased by sevenfold between 1974 and 1986.

The city schools suffer most. For example, on a single day in September 1986, 117 people were arrested in the midsize city of Passaic, New Jersey, on charges of possession of cocaine, crack, and other drugs in the playground of a local high school. Yet high school students are exposed to drugs wherever their geographical location and whatever their social class and I.Q. Urban, suburban, and rural schools alike have reported widespread drug problems among their student populations. Children with high I.Q.s often turn out to be experimenting with drugs alongside their less gifted or motivated peers. Certainly teenagers from affluent neighborhoods are as vulnerable to the lure of drug experimentation as children from low- or middle-class neighborhoods, or maybe even more so; well-to-do children have the money needed to buy drugs. Any mid-1980s high school principal who answered "no" to the question of whether drugs were available in his or her school was almost certainly untruthful or extraordinarily naive.

The Youngest Victims

Substance abuse by preteens is perhaps the most dismaying reality of the nation's drug crisis. An especially telling survey conducted by the *Weekly Reader* in 1983 gathered the opinions of 3.7 million students across the country on the subject of drugs. For the first time, children in grades 4 through 12 were interviewed regarding their opinions on drugs. In this study, students in the fourth grade said they were aware of incidents of peer pressure in which children of their age were urged to use drugs. Thirty-nine percent of children in this age group also said that "using drugs is a big problem among kids their age." One out of four fourth graders felt "some" to "a lot" of pressure to experiment with beer, wine, liquor, or marijuana.

Table 3, compiled by NIDA and released in 1981, shows the percentages of youths who were actually experimenting with drugs when still in sixth grade. Particularly disturbing is the high percentage of sixth graders who had already ex-

Grade of First Use for Sixteen Types of Drugs											
Grade in Which Drug Was First Used	Marijuana	Hallucinogens	LSD	PCP	Cocaine	Heroin	Stimulants	Sedatives	Barbiturates	Tranquilizers	Alcohol	Cigarettes
6th	1.9	0.1	0.1	0.2	0.1	0.2	0.3	0.3	0.2	0.3	8.0	3.0
7–8th	13.0	0.8	0.5	1.0	0.5	0.0	1.5	0.9	0.7	1.6	22.2	7.2
9th	16.5	2.2	1.4	1.9	1.7	0.2	4.3	2.5	2.3	3.0	24.8	5.8
10th	14.7	3.5	2.2	2.7	3.3	0.2	6.6	3.3	3.0	3.3	19.3	4.7
11th	9.7	4.3	3.3	2.6	5.8	0.2	7.3	4.8	3.2	4.4	11.9	3.4
12th	4.4	2.4	1.7	1.0	4.3	0.4	6.3	3.2	1.6	2.6	7.0	1.7
Never used	39.7	86.7	90.7	90.4	84.3	98.9	73.6	85.1	89.0	84.8	6.8	74.2

Table 3
Source: National Institute on Drug Abuse/Univ. of Michigan Institute for Social Research

perimented with alcohol, and the across-the-board increases in drug use from the sixth to the eighth grade. Clearly, alcohol and marijuana are widely used by the country's elementary and secondary school students. Given the status of these substances as "gateway" drugs, this survey presents an alarming picture indeed.

Warning Signs and Ultimate Dangers

Although it is difficult to spot an adolescent or adult who only abuses drugs and/or alcohol occasionally, the warning signs for frequent or addicted users are quite clear. Obvious physical indications include the familiar symptoms of alcohol intoxication and the telltale bloodshot eyes of someone who has recently smoked marijuana. Other symptoms of drug abuse include insomnia, unexplained weight loss, academic problems, and a sharp increase in moodiness, aggression, or withdrawal.

Overall, an adolescent with a serious drug problem may feel fundamentally alienated from his or her home environment and from one or both parents. He or she may be particularly susceptible to peer pressure and unable to cope with academic demands and social anxieties. Unable to communicate their doubts and fears to others, many of these teenagers simply retreat into a world of drugs.

The high incidence of drug use among young people in high school and college is especially troubling in view of another crisis now confronting society: a tragic increase in the rate of teenage suicide. Dr. Leighton C. Whitaker, a counselor at Swarthmore College in Pennsylvania, was quoted in the *New York Times* as citing a link between teenage suicides and what he called "the drugging of America." Fully 80% of suicide attempts among college students, according to Dr. Whitaker, take the form of a drug overdose; in 1 out of 2 cases, the substance on which the student overdoses is a prescription drug taken from parents' supplies.

In general, young people who abuse drugs may be attempting to cope with a level of anxiety or depression that is in itself presuicidal. The drug problem in these cases is only a symptom of underlying emotional problems. Then,

Drinking alcohol is the most widespread form of drug abuse among teenagers in the 1980s. Because alcohol is legal and readily available many young people are oblivious to the dangers of this addictive drug.

too, extreme abuse of certain drugs can precipitate the kinds of mental disturbances, often characterized by feelings of hopelessness and lack of control, that can lead to suicide.

Finding Solutions

In the past, schools were often at a loss when it came to dealing with drug use among school-age children. There were few coordinated efforts between the school and the home to use the classroom itself as a forum for educating young people about the effects and dangers of drugs. However, recent media attention pointing out the scope of the drug problem has finally galvanized educators and parents alike. Videotapes and other learning aids devised to prevent or curtail drug abuse among students have become widely available to schools. Moreover, after some controversy, drug education programs are now standard parts of the kindergarten through 12th grade curriculum in many school districts.

Much of the credit for making drug education a priority in the nation's schools must go to concerned parents who finally opened their eyes to the seriousness of the drug problem and decided to do something about it. Parent Alert groups have sprung up in communities all over the country. They are dedicated to creating an antidrug environment that will help to combat the peer pressure many young people feel when making decisions about drug use; that will enable parents to present a united front when it comes to forbidding the use of drugs and alcohol by young people in their homes; and that will provide the sort of support system families need to combat substance abuse problems that have already taken hold of their child.

Instances of parents themselves becoming actively involved in antidrug programs abound. For example, in *Managing the Drugs in Your Life*, Stephen Levy, Ph.D. recounts the story of a New Jersey housewife named Gerri Silverman who in 1981 began a voluntary drug education program targeted at fifth and sixth graders. The program, called "It's Your Decision," employs games and materials that educate children about drugs before they are confronted with the choice of using them. Silverman also urged her local PTA to act against drugs, and in 1982 the group initiated a "Drug Awareness Week" that incorporated walkathons, publicity, and drug

In 1986 U.S. secretary of education William J. Bennett launched a campaign against drug abuse on the nation's college campuses, saying, "drug use is open and the institutions have acquiesced in the problem."

education programs to inform parents and children of the dangers of drugs.

On a larger scale, a guidance counselor from Tampa, Florida, began a "Me-ology" program in 1979 for children in the sixth grade, to be followed up in the ninth grade. This program promotes exercises for coping with peer pressure and learning enough self-respect to deal with life without drugs. By May 1984 the successful program had moved into 9 other states and more than 300 teachers had participated in a 3-day seminar that explained the course's dynamics.

Even students have begun to relay an antidrug message to their peers. In 1979, one sixth grader, Billy Colette, began one such program for fourth, fifth, and sixth graders at his school in Florida. He received enough positive feedback to begin a high school antidrug group called Florida Informed Teens (FIT) in 1984, which eventually opened branch memberships across the state.

The flipside of incorporating "fun" into drug education is maintaining discipline in the schools when there are incidents of drug abuse. In 1977, for example, principal Bill Rudolph of Northside High in Atlanta, Georgia, informed parents and children that the school would take "necessary steps" if drug use occurred during school hours. He then proceeded to do just that. Every time a student was caught with drugs, the police were called to make an arrest. Quickly, the results of this approach could be seen. By 1982 the school reported only one drug-related incident during its entire school year.

A man begs for money on a city street. Drug use abounds in both urban and rural areas of the United States, but the drug trade is centered in the poverty-stricken areas of major cities.

CHAPTER 7

DOWN AND OUT IN
THE INNER CITY

Drug use and abuse is a universal phenomenon, as common in posh prep schools as in city high schools, and as likely to appear in rural Kansas as in downtown Los Angeles. But in the United States, the drug trade is still centered in the cities. In those locations the dealers do their business, the middle- and upper-class users go for their fixes, and the true down-and-outers try to satisfy their continual cravings.

Every large city has its share of centers for the drug trade. New York City's Washington Square Park typifies both the frenzy and the quiet desperation that attend drug deals in such locations. Centered in trendy Greenwich Village and abutting New York University, the park is, according to local police and other city authorities, one of the most blatant of all urban drug markets.

For pedestrians strolling through, the park resembles a Middle Eastern bazaar — except that only one type of commodity is for sale. Drug dealers offer passers-by and riders in passing cars a wide array of wares including marijuana, heroin, amphetamines, and crack. Small-time dealers collect their supplies out of sight of the ever-present police patrols and fan out to entice more customers. Customers in well-tailored

An aerial view of New York City's Washington Square Park, one of the nation's most blatant drug-dealing centers.

suits mix with flamboyantly dressed dealers and ragged bums as they try to make their drug connections without appearing to be too noticeable. And the local residents try to avoid walking through the park, especially at night.

But Washington Square Park is a paradise compared with New York City's Washington Heights. There, in the center of the ghetto, drug dealers abound, selling to locals and residents of the New York and New Jersey suburbs who drive through briefly in their automobiles. In one 4-month period in 1986, police made 3,000 drug-related arrests in Washington Heights.

Parents of teenagers in such areas must fear not only that their children will become drug users but also that they will become lookouts or runners for drug dealers. The incentive to do so is strong. Dealers are reputed to offer youngsters hundreds of dollars a week to work for them. One drug trafficking ring in Boston had so much cash flowing in that it was able to operate much like a legitimate business. It gave its employees — dealers, couriers, and "baby sitters," who guarded drugs in "stash houses" — paid vacations, used a toll-free phone number for orders, and entered noncompetition agreements with other drug dealers in the area. "You see how much money they have, the cars they own, the girls they attract," explained one ninth grader. "The people who have most around here are the druggies."

Robert Israel, a former high school teacher, outlined the extent of the problem in *Boston* magazine. "I remember an afternoon," he wrote, "when I found two of my delinquent students on Sonoma Street. They were working as lookouts at a shooting gallery, keeping watch for the police while junkies went inside to mainline heroin. I brought them back to school, but they were incensed. 'We're making more money on Sonoma Street in a week than we make at our work sites in a year,' the students told me."

The Downward Path to Addiction

Drug dealers routinely target youngsters in an effort to ensnare them in drug dealing and abuse. One girl recalls her teenage years in a rundown part of Brooklyn, New York. "Pushers were giving kids heroin for free," she relates.

A burned-out house in a run-down section of Brooklyn, New York. Children who live in such areas can become victims of drug pushers who profit from addicting new customers.

"They'd give them a skin pop for nothing. It's a great marketing technique. It's no different from when you go into a supermarket and some guy hands you little samples of candy to taste. It works. The pushers give the kids a little bit of cocaine, they give them a little taste of crack, and start the kids off for nothing. Before long, the kids are hooked."

All too often, it is a short step from user to dealer in these situations. Many young people, including minors, turn to dealing in order to continue raising the money to support expensive drug habits. Nor is drug dealing the only crime attempted by these individuals; robbery, assault, and prostitution have all been linked to people looking for money to buy drugs. The book *Crime and Human Nature* (1985) by James Q. Wilson and Richard J. Herrnstein cited a study in which a group of 239 male subjects in Miami, Florida, admitted that they had committed an average of 337 crimes each during the preceding year. Half of these crimes were drug sales. A 1986 study in Manhattan of adult men arrested for serious crimes indicated that 78% were cocaine users. In Los Angeles, California, an increase in criminal juvenile violence led to a comment from the local police force that a rise in homicides in Los Angeles resulted from "territorial disputes among gangs who all want the privilege of selling cocaine."

At its worst, being "hooked" marks the start of a descent into a hell in which drugs dominate every waking moment. John, a recovering addict in the Northeast, remembered some of his life as a full-blown addict. "My life was definitely centered on alcohol and drugs," he said. "I was always on speed when I was working, and I performed very well. After a while, I couldn't work unless I had it. I took speed every day, and I drank every day. Alcohol and drugs did everything for me. They calmed me down, made me sociable, made me funny. They made me all the things I wanted to be and couldn't act out.

"I tried heroin. I don't know why anyone would want to do that. Heroin is a terrible thing. You could be sitting there and someone's nailing your mother to a wall and you'll say: 'Well, maybe I'll give her a hand down.' Nothing makes any difference.

"I'd mix anything — beer, whiskey, pills. I never wanted to quit."

Chuck Diedrich, the founder of Synanon. This drug-treatment program has been criticized for being cultlike and overly authoritarian, but it has nonetheless scored numerous successes in the battle against addiction.

Getting Another Chance

Drug rehabilitation programs such as Horizon House, Phoenix House, Odyssey House, and Synanon, all located in major cities across the United States, offer the destitute urban addict, as well as his more affluent peers, another chance. These programs provide intensive psychotherapy and vocational training in an effort to help addicts "kick" their habits. Living at a treatment center is one way for the addict to escape the temptation of living and dealing with drugs on the street.

Unfortunately, rehabilitation centers in the inner city are not always accessible to the addict. Waiting lists for these programs are long and constantly growing. Federal and state funds to support these centers vary from year to year. And the fact remains that once a person willingly enters into an existence defined by drug use, crime, and often poverty, the odds of escaping dim considerably, no matter what aid is offered. Tragically, far too many users in this category never really look for that second chance.

President Ronald Reagan signs an antidrug bill into law in September 1986. The law focuses on strengthening penalties for manufacturing, selling, and using illicit substances.

CHAPTER 8

SIGNS OF HOPE

No sooner does one drug dominate public consciousness than another appears on the streets, unannounced and mysterious. As long as it does not take too many lives, the new drug then becomes the recreational substance of choice for a new generation of users.

In the late 1800s, excitement centered around cocaine. In the Prohibition era of the 1920s, alcohol was the rage. LSD became the focus of interest in the 1960s, followed soon by speed, PCP, and other concoctions. In the 1980s, cocaine once again came to the fore. Throughout, marijuana remained a stable starter drug, along with alcohol, for young initiates. And basement chemists have continued to devise new means of providing customers with their highs while keeping clear of the authorities with the development of so-called designer drugs.

Public attitudes toward drug use also undergo drastic swings of the pendulum. The enthusiasm for cocaine expressed by the medical profession in the late 19th century gave way to widespread efforts to ban that drug in the early 1900s. America's long love affair with alcohol seemed to peak in the era of Prohibition and then to decline somewhat in the following years. The free and easy "turn on, tune in, drop out" days of the 1960s were followed by the antidrug reaction of the middle 1980s.

Currently, the public is loudly proclaiming an intolerance for illicit drugs and a healthy suspicion of prescription drugs. The campaign against drugs in the middle 1980s has developed a double focus. One goal is to identify the worst drug abusers and help them through a variety of treatment programs. The other goal is to prevent the young from starting to use drugs. These two aims have been promoted in a number of national, statewide, and local antidrug programs.

The War Against Drugs

In 1982, President Ronald Reagan called for a broad-based national program against drugs. In a series of aggressive moves, his administration established a Drug Abuse Policy Office that, in turn, put together a federal strategy concerning drug abuse prevention and rehabilitation in the United States. The president requested and received from Congress $901.4 million to support federal and state drug abuse programs in 1983. Nine Cabinet departments and thirty-three federal agencies were recruited for further involvement in this program. Finally, stricter laws regarding prosecution and punishment of drug smugglers entering the country's borders were promoted vigorously by federal authorities.

States have also enacted laws and programs aimed at reducing or eliminating drug- and alcohol-related incidents among their respective populations. One of the most impressive results emerged from decisions in several states to increase the drinking age in an effort to reduce the number of deaths resulting from drunk driving. New York and New Jersey, 2 of the first states to increase legal drinking ages from 18 to 21, reported that the number of accidents involving drivers under 21 declined by more than 40% in the years after those actions. Studies in other states revealed lower but still impressive reductions of between 10 and 20% in death tolls. Obviously, an effective response to drunk driving was being carried out with the widespread support of the general public.

Other efforts to control the abuse of illegal drugs by federal and state authorities caused controversy, however. A campaign by New York City police to impound the automobiles of individuals trying to buy drugs in the city elicited strong complaints from suburban parents whose teenagers

New Yorkers turned out in full force for this March on Drugs parade in 1970. The march was billed as the first antidrug festival.

returned home without the family car. A major effort by the Reagan administration in 1986 to require all government workers to undergo urinalysis to detect the presence of drugs was excoriated as an abuse of these individuals' civil rights.

Clearly, officials in all areas are still trying to develop effective ways of discouraging drug use. While some strides have been made, much more coordination and planning, to say nothing of money and manpower, are needed.

Frontline Commandos

The most persuasive antidrug campaigners are those who have been there — former addicts and recovering addicts. Because they know the craving for cocaine, heroin, or alcohol, they can empathize with the feelings of current addicts. Former addicts were recruited to participate in a statewide antidrug program, serving on New York State's Street Research Unit.

These reformed users often patrol the streets of New York City to keep an eye on the overall drug scene. Dressed for the part, they infiltrate crack dens, shooting galleries, and dealing sites in an effort to spot potentially dangerous trends in drug abuse long before the police can do so.

"They [former addicts] are my frontline commandos," said Julio M. Martinez, executive director of New York State's Division of Substance Abuse. "I established the unit because we can't afford to get caught by surprise and learn about a drug problem from emergency room data and from deaths."

Some of the most positive victories in the war against drugs have been made by private citizens who volunteer their own time and energies speaking out against drugs. Many former addicts speak before audiences of young people, hoping that the stories of their own suffering will dissuade others from the temptations of drugs.

A former drug addict speaks about his experiences. Recovering addicts are among the most ardent — and persuasive — antidrug campaigners.

Bob Patterson, Stanley Boyd, and Michael Burns, for example, make a strong case against drugs when they visit seventh and eighth graders in Everett, Massachusetts, a working-class town just north of Boston. All three men are in wheelchairs as a result of drug abuse. Patterson celebrated his 17th birthday by drinking beer, whiskey, and cough medicine. The near-lethal "cocktail" put him into a coma from which he has only partly recovered. Boyd overdosed on cocaine and other illicit drugs; now he is a paraplegic who cannot use his legs or even speak. Burns, driving his car while high on drugs, was in an accident in which he sustained paralyzing injuries.

Antidrug programs initiated by parents, students, and teachers only a few years ago also continue to make strides among children on all school levels. Creators of these programs continue to be encouraged by the positive response children and teenagers have to drug education. Teachers who are former addicts can play an especially strong role in persuading those younger than themselves not to start taking drugs, or if they have started, to stop. Martin Finnegan, the athletic director of a New England high school, can recall the exact time, to the minute, at which he took his last drink. He had been a "problem drinker" before he realized that he was an alcoholic and sought treatment. As he recovered, he sought to share his experience with teenagers and to encourage them and their parents to realize the dangers of drug and alcohol abuse.

Such talks provide benefits for those who give them as well as the students at whom they are aimed. "Recovering abusers get a chance to regain a sense of worth and feel part of the community again by telling their stories," said Susan Griffin, founder of a group known as Street Smarts that educates students about drug abuse. "They also reinforce their own needs for sobriety; they tell kids, 'We don't want what happened to us to happen to you.'"

Fighting on Many Fronts

As mentioned in previous chapters, the need for drug education is not limited to any age group. As new combinations of drugs emerge on the market, there may be increasing experimentation and a growing number of tragic addictions in all segments of society. On a more positive note, antidrug

A meeting of Amethyst, a support group for women alcoholics. Programs such as this make it easier for drug-dependent people to get help and therefore play an important role in the battle for a drug-free society.

programs are becoming visible in the most unexpected places.

Corporations large and small are opening their own chapters of Alcoholics Anonymous and Narcotics Anonymous, encouraging addicts to seek company-paid treatment, and helping to smooth the return of the rehabilitated addicts to day-to-day life in the workplace. *Managing the Drugs in Your Life* quotes an official formerly affiliated with the federal government's Alcohol, Drug Abuse and Mental Health Association as stating that from 1972 to 1982 company-sponsored EAPs grew from fewer than 300 to more than 5,500 across the country.

"Twelve percent of all U.S. firms have EAPs and seventy percent of these programs now assist in problems of drug abuse as well as alcohol abuse," the official stated in the early 1980s. "Trends indicate that these figures may have increased substantially since that time."

"The experts are saying that twenty percent of the work force is having problems with drugs," echoed Jean Hails, national president of Associated Builders and Contractors, a group of small companies that has taken the lead in treating on-the-job drug and alcohol abusers. "It's time that business got involved."

The theme of tackling drug abuse wherever it surfaces has also emerged in many of America's inner cities. Led by clergy from local churches, growing numbers of neighborhood groups have started to track down the crack houses, shooting galleries, and other centers of the drug dealing trade in attempts to beat back the onslaught of drugs by force of numbers and moral authority. Leaders of the movement admit that they will never remove drug deals and dealers entirely from their neighborhoods. But by forcing them to move from place to place, the leaders hope to slow the growth of the inner-city drug trade.

Conclusion

Who uses drugs? Sadly, the answer seems to encompass a broad cross section of our entire society. No longer can substance abuse be written off as a ghetto disease, or even as a pastime of writers, artists, and others outside the mainstream of convention. This is a country where top executives buy and use cocaine during their lunch hours; where factory workers show up for work too hung over to perform their jobs adequately; where physicians and nurses medicate themselves with the prescription drugs they are supposed to use to heal others; where athletic superstars and beloved performers routinely are exposed as having problems with chemical dependency; and, perhaps most alarmingly, where a generation of young people puts its future at risk in pursuit of drug- and alcohol-induced "highs."

But it would seem that the nation may have reached a turning point when it comes to drug and alcohol misuse. Efforts to combat the epidemic are gaining momentum at the grassroots level, in the schools, among professional organizations, within specific companies and industries, and in state and national legislative forums. The most successful weapon against this national crisis is education. The more information people have about the effects of the toxic chemicals so many of them are ingesting and the agonies of addiction, the more hope there is for a drug-free society.

APPENDIX

State Agencies
for the Prevention and Treatment
of Drug Abuse

ALABAMA
Department of Mental Health
Division of Mental Illness and
  Substance Abuse Community
  Programs
200 Interstate Park Drive
P.O. Box 3710
Montgomery, AL 36193
(205) 271-9253

ALASKA
Department of Health and Social
  Services
Office of Alcoholism and Drug
  Abuse
Pouch H-05-F
Juneau, AK 99811
(907) 586-6201

ARIZONA
Department of Health Services
Division of Behavioral Health
  Services
Bureau of Community Services
Alcohol Abuse and Alcoholism
  Section
2500 East Van Buren
Phoenix, AZ 85008
(602) 255-1238

Department of Health Services
Division of Behavioral Health
  Services
Bureau of Community Services
Drug Abuse Section
2500 East Van Buren
Phoenix, AZ 85008
(602) 255-1240

ARKANSAS
Department of Human Services
Office of Alcohol and Drug Abuse
  Prevention
1515 West 7th Avenue
Suite 310
Little Rock, AR 72202
(501) 371-2603

CALIFORNIA
Department of Alcohol and Drug
  Abuse
111 Capitol Mall
Sacramento, CA 95814
(916) 445-1940

COLORADO
Department of Health
Alcohol and Drug Abuse Division
4210 East 11th Avenue
Denver, CO 80220
(303) 320-6137

CONNECTICUT
Alcohol and Drug Abuse
  Commission
999 Asylum Avenue
3rd Floor
Hartford, CT 06105
(203) 566-4145

DELAWARE
Division of Mental Health
Bureau of Alcoholism and Drug
  Abuse
1901 North Dupont Highway
Newcastle, DE 19720
(302) 421-6101

DISTRICT OF COLUMBIA
Department of Human Services
Office of Health Planning and
   Development
601 Indiana Avenue, NW
Suite 500
Washington, D.C. 20004
(202) 724-5641

FLORIDA
Department of Health and
   Rehabilitative Services
Alcoholic Rehabilitation Program
1317 Winewood Boulevard
Room 187A
Tallahassee, FL 32301
(904) 488-0396

Department of Health and
   Rehabilitative Services
Drug Abuse Program
1317 Winewood Boulevard
Building 6, Room 155
Tallahassee, FL 32301
(904) 488-0900

GEORGIA
Department of Human Resources
Division of Mental Health and
   Mental Retardation
Alcohol and Drug Section
618 Ponce De Leon Avenue, NE
Atlanta, GA 30365-2101
(404) 894-4785

HAWAII
Department of Health
Mental Health Division
Alcohol and Drug Abuse Branch
1250 Punch Bowl Street
P.O. Box 3378
Honolulu, HI 96801
(808) 548-4280

IDAHO
Department of Health and Welfare
Bureau of Preventive Medicine
Substance Abuse Section
450 West State
Boise, ID 83720
(208) 334-4368

ILLINOIS
Department of Mental Health and
   Developmental Disabilities
Division of Alcoholism
160 North La Salle Street
Room 1500
Chicago, IL 60601
(312) 793-2907

Illinois Dangerous Drugs
   Commission
300 North State Street
Suite 1500
Chicago, IL 60610
(312) 822-9860

INDIANA
Department of Mental Health
Division of Addiction Services
429 North Pennsylvania Street
Indianapolis, IN 46204
(317) 232-7816

IOWA
Department of Substance Abuse
505 5th Avenue
Insurance Exchange Building
Suite 202
Des Moines, IA 50319
(515) 281-3641

KANSAS
Department of Social Rehabilitation
Alcohol and Drug Abuse Services
2700 West 6th Street
Biddle Building
Topeka, KS 66606
(913) 296-3925

KENTUCKY
Cabinet for Human Resources
Department of Health Services
Substance Abuse Branch
275 East Main Street
Frankfort, KY 40601
(502) 564-2880

LOUISIANA
Department of Health and Human
 Resources
Office of Mental Health and
 Substance Abuse
655 North 5th Street
P.O. Box 4049
Baton Rouge, LA 70821
(504) 342-2565

MAINE
Department of Human Services
Office of Alcoholism and Drug
 Abuse Prevention
Bureau of Rehabilitation
32 Winthrop Street
Augusta, ME 04330
(207) 289-2781

MARYLAND
Alcoholism Control Administration
201 West Preston Street
Fourth Floor
Baltimore, MD 21201
(301) 383-2977

State Health Department
Drug Abuse Administration
201 West Preston Street
Baltimore, MD 21201
(301) 383-3312

MASSACHUSETTS
Department of Public Health
Division of Alcoholism
755 Boylston Street
Sixth Floor
Boston, MA 02116
(617) 727-1960

Department of Public Health
Division of Drug Rehabilitation
600 Washington Street
Boston, MA 02114
(617) 727-8617

MICHIGAN
Department of Public Health
Office of Substance Abuse Services
3500 North Logan Street
P.O. Box 30035
Lansing, MI 48909
(517) 373-8603

MINNESOTA
Department of Public Welfare
Chemical Dependency Program
 Division
Centennial Building
658 Cedar Street
4th Floor
Saint Paul, MN 55155
(612) 296-4614

MISSISSIPPI
Department of Mental Health
Division of Alcohol and Drug Abuse
1102 Robert E. Lee Building
Jackson, MS 39201
(601) 359-1297

MISSOURI
Department of Mental Health
Division of Alcoholism and Drug
 Abuse
2002 Missouri Boulevard
P.O. Box 687
Jefferson City, MO 65102
(314) 751-4942

MONTANA
Department of Institutions
Alcohol and Drug Abuse Division
1539 11th Avenue
Helena, MT 59620
(406) 449-2827

NEBRASKA
Department of Public Institutions
Division of Alcoholism and Drug
Abuse
801 West Van Dorn Street
P.O. Box 94728
Lincoln, NB 68509
(402) 471-2851, Ext. 415

NEVADA
Department of Human Resources
Bureau of Alcohol and Drug Abuse
505 East King Street
Carson City, NV 89710
(702) 885-4790

NEW HAMPSHIRE
Department of Health and Welfare
Office of Alcohol and Drug Abuse
    Prevention
Hazen Drive
Health and Welfare Building
Concord, NH 03301
(603) 271-4627

NEW JERSEY
Department of Health
Division of Alcoholism
129 East Hanover Street CN 362
Trenton, NJ 08625
(609) 292-8949

Department of Health
Division of Narcotic and Drug
    Abuse Control
129 East Hanover Street CN 362
Trenton, NJ 08625
(609) 292-8949

NEW MEXICO
Health and Environment Department
Behavioral Services Division
Substance Abuse Bureau
725 Saint Michaels Drive
P.O. Box 968
Santa Fe, NM 87503
(505) 984-0020, Ext. 304

NEW YORK
Division of Alcoholism and Alcohol
    Abuse
194 Washington Avenue
Albany, NY 12210
(518) 474-5417

Division of Substance Abuse
    Services
Executive Park South
Box 8200
Albany, NY 12203
(518) 457-7629

NORTH CAROLINA
Department of Human Resources
Division of Mental Health, Mental
    Retardation and Substance Abuse
    Services
Alcohol and Drug Abuse Services
325 North Salisbury Street
Albemarle Building
Raleigh, NC 27611
(919) 733-4670

NORTH DAKOTA
Department of Human Services
Division of Alcoholism and Drug
    Abuse
State Capitol Building
Bismarck, ND 58505
(701) 224-2767

OHIO
Department of Health
Division of Alcoholism
246 North High Street
P.O. Box 118
Columbus, OH 43216
(614) 466-3543

Department of Mental Health
Bureau of Drug Abuse
65 South Front Street
Columbus, OH 43215
(614) 466-9023

OKLAHOMA
Department of Mental Health
Alcohol and Drug Programs
4545 North Lincoln Boulevard
Suite 100 East Terrace
P.O. Box 53277
Oklahoma City, OK 73152
(405) 521-0044

OREGON
Department of Human Resources
Mental Health Division
Office of Programs for Alcohol and
    Drug Problems
2575 Bittern Street, NE
Salem, OR 97310
(503) 378-2163

PENNSYLVANIA
Department of Health
Office of Drug and Alcohol
    Programs
Commonwealth and Forster Avenues
Health and Welfare Building
P.O. Box 90
Harrisburg, PA 17108
(717) 787-9857

RHODE ISLAND
Department of Mental Health,
    Mental Retardation and Hospitals
Division of Substance Abuse
Substance Abuse Administration
    Building
Cranston, RI 02920
(401) 464-2091

SOUTH CAROLINA
Commission on Alcohol and Drug
    Abuse
3700 Forest Drive
Columbia, SC 29204
(803) 758-2521

SOUTH DAKOTA
Department of Health
Division of Alcohol and Drug Abuse
523 East Capitol, Joe Foss Building
Pierre, SD 57501
(605) 773-4806

TENNESSEE
Department of Mental Health and
    Mental Retardation
Alcohol and Drug Abuse Services
505 Deaderick Street
James K. Polk Building,
    Fourth Floor
Nashville, TN 37219
(615) 741-1921

TEXAS
Commission on Alcoholism
809 Sam Houston State Office
    Building
Austin, TX 78701
(512) 475-2577
Department of Community Affairs
Drug Abuse Prevention Division
2015 South Interstate Highway 35
P.O. Box 13166
Austin, TX 78711
(512) 443-4100

UTAH
Department of Social Services
Division of Alcoholism and Drugs
150 West North Temple
Suite 350
P.O. Box 2500
Salt Lake City, UT 84110
(801) 533-6532

VERMONT
Agency of Human Services
Department of Social and
    Rehabilitation Services
Alcohol and Drug Abuse Division
103 South Main Street
Waterbury, VT 05676
(802) 241-2170

VIRGINIA
Department of Mental Health and
  Mental Retardation
Division of Substance Abuse
109 Governor Street
P.O. Box 1797
Richmond, VA 23214
(804) 786-5313

WASHINGTON
Department of Social and Health
  Service
Bureau of Alcohol and Substance
  Abuse
Office Building—44 W
Olympia, WA 98504
(206) 753-5866

WEST VIRGINIA
Department of Health
Office of Behavioral Health Services
Division on Alcoholism and Drug
  Abuse
1800 Washington Street East
Building 3 Room 451
Charleston, WV 25305
(304) 348-2276

WISCONSIN
Department of Health and Social
  Services
Division of Community Services
Bureau of Community Programs
Alcohol and Other Drug Abuse
  Program Office
1 West Wilson Street
P.O. Box 7851
Madison, WI 53707
(608) 266-2717

WYOMING
Alcohol and Drug Abuse Programs
Hathaway Building
Cheyenne, WY 82002
(307) 777-7115, Ext. 7118

GUAM
Mental Health & Substance Abuse
  Agency
P.O. Box 20999
Guam 96921

PUERTO RICO
Department of Addiction Control
  Services
Alcohol Abuse Programs
P.O. Box B-Y Rio Piedras Station
Rio Piedras, PR 00928
(809) 763-5014

Department of Addiction Control
  Services
Drug Abuse Programs
P.O. Box B-Y Rio Piedras Station
Rio Piedras, PR 00928
(809) 764-8140

VIRGIN ISLANDS
Division of Mental Health,
  Alcoholism & Drug Dependency
  Services
P.O. Box 7329
Saint Thomas, Virgin Islands 00801
(809) 774-7265

AMERICAN SAMOA
LBJ Tropical Medical Center
Department of Mental Health Clinic
Pago Pago, American Samoa 96799

TRUST TERRITORIES
Director of Health Services
Office of the High Commissioner
Saipan, Trust Territories 96950

Further Reading

Herrnstein, Richard J., and James Q. Wilson. *Crime and Human Nature*. New York: Simon and Schuster, 1985.

Levy, Stephen. *Managing the Drugs in Your Life*. New York: McGraw-Hill, 1983.

Malone, Michael S. *The Big Story: The Billion Dollar Story of Silicon Valley*. New York: Doubleday, 1985.

Mann, Peggy. *Marijuana Alert*. New York: McGraw-Hill, 1984.

Morse, Donald Ray, and M. Lawrence Furst. *Women Under Stress*. New York: Van Nostrand Reinhold Co., 1981.

Norris, William. *The Upstate Sky*. New York: W. W. Norton and Co., 1981.

Quinnett, Paul G. *The Troubled People Book*. New York: Continuum, 1982.

Glossary

addiction a condition caused by repeated drug use, characterized by a compulsive urge to continue using the drug, a tendency to increase the dosage, and physiological and/or psychological dependence

amphetamine a drug that stimulates the central nervous system, alleviates fatigue, and produces a feeling of alertness and well-being. Although it has been used for weight control, repeated use of the drug can cause restlessness and insomnia

anesthetic a drug that produces a loss of sensation or consciousness; can be local or general

barbiturates drugs that have a depressant effect on the central nervous system and respiration. They have toxic side effects and, when used excessively, can lead to tolerance, dependence, and even death

cocaine the primary psychoactive ingredient in the coca plant and a behavioral stimulant

crack a less expensive, highly addictive form of cocaine

detoxification the process by which an addicted individual is gradually withdrawn from the abused drug, usually under medical supervision and sometimes in conjunction with the administration of other drugs

heroin a semisynthetic opiate produced by a chemical modification of morphine

LSD lysergic acid diethylamide; a hallucinogen derived from a fungus that grows on rye or from morning glory seeds

marijuana a psychoactive substance with the active ingredient THC, found in the crushed leaves, flowers, and branches of the hemp plant

mescaline a psychedelic drug found in the peyote cactus

methadone a synthetic opiate producing effects similar to morphine; used to treat pain associated with terminal cancer and in the treatment of heroin addiction

morphine an opiate used as a sedative and pain reliever

narcotics originally, a group of drugs producing effects similar to morphine; often used to refer to any substance that sedates, has a depressive effect, and/or causes dependence

opiates compounds from the milky juice of the poppy plant *Papaver somniferum*, including opium, morphine, codeine, and their derivatives (such as heroin)

PCP also called phencyclidine; an illicit drug used for its stimulating, depressing, and/or hallucinogenic effects

physical dependence adaption of the body to the presence of a drug such that its absence produces withdrawal symptoms

psychological dependence a condition in which the drug user craves a drug to maintain a sense of well-being and feels discomfort when deprived of it

sedative a drug that produces calmness, relaxation, and sleep; barbiturates are considered sedatives

stimulant any drug that increases brain activity and produces the sensation of greater energy, euphoria, and increased alertness

synthesize creating a chemical compound by combining elements or simpler compounds or by degrading a complex compound; generally refers to a laboratory process

tolerance a decrease of susceptibility to the effects of a drug due to its continued administration, resulting in the user's need to increase the dosage to achieve the effects experienced previously

tranquilizer an antianxiety drug that has calming and relaxing effects; Librium and Valium are tranquilizers

Valium trade name for diazepam, a benzodiazepine or minor tranquilizer

withdrawal the physiological and psychological effects of discontinued usage of drugs

PICTURE CREDITS

Index

Peter Gwynne is the director of editorial operations for *The Scientist* in Washington, D.C. His work in the science field has appeared in *High Technology, Technology Review,* and *Newsweek,* where he also served as science editor. Mr. Gwynne was the recipient of the 1986 Aviation-Space Writers Association Award.

Solomon H. Snyder, M.D. is Distinguished Service Professor of Neuroscience, Pharmacology and Psychiatry at The Johns Hopkins University School of Medicine. He has served as president of the Society for Neuroscience and in 1978 received the Albert Lasker Award in Medical Research. He has authored *Uses of Marijuana, Madness and the Brain, The Troubled Mind, Biological Aspects of Mental Disorder,* and edited *Perspective in Neuropharmacology: A Tribute to Julius Axelrod.* Professor Snyder was a research associate with Dr. Axelrod at the National Institutes of Health.

Barry L. Jacobs, Ph.D., is currently a professor in the program of neuroscience at Princeton University. Professor Jacobs is author of *Serotonin Neurotransmission and Behavior* and *Hallucinogens: Neurochemical, Behavioral and Clinical Perspectives.* He has written many journal articles in the field of neuroscience and contributed numerous chapters to books on behavior and brain science. He has been a member of several panels of the National Institute of Mental Health.

Joann Ellison Rodgers, M.S. (Columbia), became Deputy Director of Public Affairs and Director of Media Relations for the Johns Hopkins Medical Institutions in Baltimore, Maryland, in 1984 after 18 years as an award-winning science journalist and widely read columnist for the Hearst newspapers.